"Pamela Capone must be a riot at parties. She can turn the most mundane details of a day into witty poetry, and find a way to connect it all to God's higher plan for us. From the mini-essays in this collection, it is clear that Pam is the kind of woman you'd want in your corner when you're in trouble to say just the right thing and help you laugh along the way…Some details of Pam's life are repeated motifs—her adoption into an Italian-American family at a young age, her children, her charity work—but her voice, rather than her situations, really drive the stories."
   IndieReader

"Messages of faith sprinkled throughout will appeal to readers with connections to the Christian tradition, but they're handled with subtlety, so readers of other persuasions can still enjoy the work.…Capone's gregarious, approachable voice allows her to deftly handle a broad variety of subjects. Rather than dwelling on misery and mishaps, the collection calls attention to the glimmers of hope and humor that lie in life's challenging moments. An upbeat, honest celebration of imperfection that makes a compelling case for the power of accepting oneself, warts and all."
   Kirkus Reviews

"Even when cracking jokes, Capone is gentle, often poking fun at herself for small offenses fed by insensitivity. As the book progresses, the author's personality becomes its primary strength, a situation not unlike a celebrity's or comedian's collection, and the author's experience with stand-up comedy may factor in. Though many vignettes also deal with serious or sad subjects, the majority cast the author's life in a humorous light. The book's editorial style engages with wordplay, including puns, and is at its strongest when delivering jokes. *I Punched Myself in the Eye* is a family-oriented book most likely to appeal to Christians. Easily read in a series of short sittings, or in one long one, this collection of short-short essays easily punches above its weight."
   Foreword **Clarion Reviews**

"In this engagingly written, faith-based essay collection, Pamela Capone finds the humor and grace in ordinary —and sometimes extraordinary— situations. Capone has coined the term, 'messay' for her prose, a combination of 'messy (informal untidy, embarrassing, difficult)' and 'essay.'…More than a few of the essays are poignant and thoughtful, rather than out-and-out funny—albeit

i

handled with Capone's appealing light touch and conversational style…Adopted at 18 months by her foster parents, after her birth parents were charged with child neglect, Capone writes many of the essays as reverent tributes to the parents who raised her and to her birth siblings, with whom she has a special bond. She also writes about her work at a girls' school in Guatemala and about helping in Haiti after the 2010 earthquake."
BlueInk Review

"Any readers out there who need a good belly laugh? Pamela Capone's latest work, *I Punched Myself in the Eye* is just the tonic for any reader looking for a fun book to pick up. This is a sparky collection of sketches drawn from everyday life: by turns hilarious, familiar, heart-warming and heart-rending. It's a book the reader can dip into at leisure, enjoying the bite-sized chapters in any order. This is observational comedy in a very human style, and the readers (be they male or female) will surely find themselves laughing or crying out loud along with the author as she regales us with her witty prose…

"Capone's ability to, as she says herself, 'admit we don't have all the answers' is very endearing, and her willingness to expose her own foibles and shortcomings is something readers will most certainly appreciate. Genuine laugh-out-loud humor is a more and more rare thing to come across in books these days, and the author takes readers back to the era of 'I Love Lucy' and the kind of selfless comedy that audiences used to enjoy on a regular basis once upon a time. Effortless writing in the dialogue in every story helps to make this a smooth read, while characterization is rounded, well-observed and vivid…

"'I'm all about *carpe diem*, I have the tattoo!' Capone cries out—and on the strength of this well-crafted book that just about sums her up."
Self-Publishing Review

"A mixture of Erma Bombeck and Barbara Johnson, yet quintessentially Pamela Capone, this collection of personal anecdotes, life lessons, and poignant observations moves the reader from smiles to laughter to tears and all stops in between. Capone's short essays are told with grace-fueled wit that will lift your spirits, stir your heart, and inspire your better self."
Robyn Henk, author of *BLESSED, Discovering God's Bigger Dream for You*

"Stunningly potent! Hilarious! Beware, Pamela Capone's brilliant ability to seize mundane happenings of life and turn them into humorous, relatable, and insightful living will provoke laugh-out-loud moments. Her unexpected honesty and fresh ways to look at life and faith challenged me how I can do likewise. This book is relevant and important for today's generation."

Tina Sechrist Randy, cofounder of IMA Guatemala

"In *I Punched Myself in the Eye,* Capone writes with equal parts humor and heart. She is your funniest friend, the one who's able to see beyond the sadness, anger, embarrassment, or public humiliation to point out, impishly, the comedy that invariably lies beneath. Her wit is never mean or cheap; rather, she mines every situation to find her own humanity and spirit. Capone uses humor to heal."

Kirsten Mickelwait, author of *Under a Vanilla Moon*

"Pamela Capone's personal 'messays' are winsome, brave, honest, real, and hilarious. She has such a unique ability to combine humor, wisdom, and pathos. Page after page, she managed to make me smile, laugh out loud, think, and feel deeply. *I Punched Myself in the Eye* will capture many hearts and minds, as I see a wide audience for this book. The woman's a truth teller, and we are wise to listen."

Dee Eastman, Daniel Plan Director

"*I Punched Myself in the Eye* is philosophically funny and provides a mature message with mischievous flair. Capone uses puns, idioms, and faux pas with artistic magnetism. Her stories will entertain with simplicity yet challenge the reader to consider living differently based upon her divine encounters with a faithful God."

Jim McNeff, author of *The Spirit Behind Badge 145*

"Capone is an entertaining storyteller-come-friend, sitting across the kitchen table with coffee in hand, sharing anecdotes of a day in the life of an ordinary wife, mother, and struggling actress with a sense of humor. Divvied up into easy-to-read vignettes, you'll chuckle too."

Janice Mock, author of *Not All Bad Comes to Harm You: Observations of a Cancer Survivor*

"There are few souls who know how to capture a scene, a feeling of being present in the very moment, in such a way as to make you really believe you were there—or wish you were. Pamela Capone is such an author. In *I Punched Myself In the Eye*, there is no shortage of moments that can tickle your funny bone, splitting your sides with laughter, and then bring you to tears. She has a gift for evoking feelings (including sadness and joy) in the reader, as well as inspiring one to be a better human being. Her warmth, her wit and wisdom and insight, are found on every page. We see in her words our own frailties, our own struggles, our own human condition. There is a unique ease about the way these stories are woven strand by strand into a tapestry against a wider backdrop of love, vulnerability, strength, and the joy of being alive. I highly recommend this book to all. It may just help you see your own life with new eyes and appreciation."

Elizabeth Midgley, author of *Families Together* and *Daily Discoveries*

"When it comes to good fiction, you expect to be entertained—to laugh, to cry, to be inspired. It's rare, though, when this happens in a collection of personal essays. In Pamela Capone's *I Punched Myself in the Eye*, you're treated to a collection of experiences that touch on the important things in life. The magic of this book is Capone's ability to treat you with an often-funny, always-spiritual ride with each story. Like *Aesop's Fables*, you'll enjoy a nice story and then realize there's a profound message hiding underneath. Read this book. A personal change for the better will be the result."

Michael Sean Marshall, author of *A Council of Angels*

"I adore Pamela Capone's sense of humor and regard her as a diamond in the writing industry. Her writings here are relatable and fun-loving. We can all associate with her knee-jerk reactions to everyday interactions with others. After dipping your toes into the refreshing shallow end, stay tuned for more of a reveal of what Pamela is all about. You will be a better person for knowing the whole Pamela Capone. I know I am."

Terri Green, author of *Simple Acts of Kindness*

I Punched Myself in the Eye

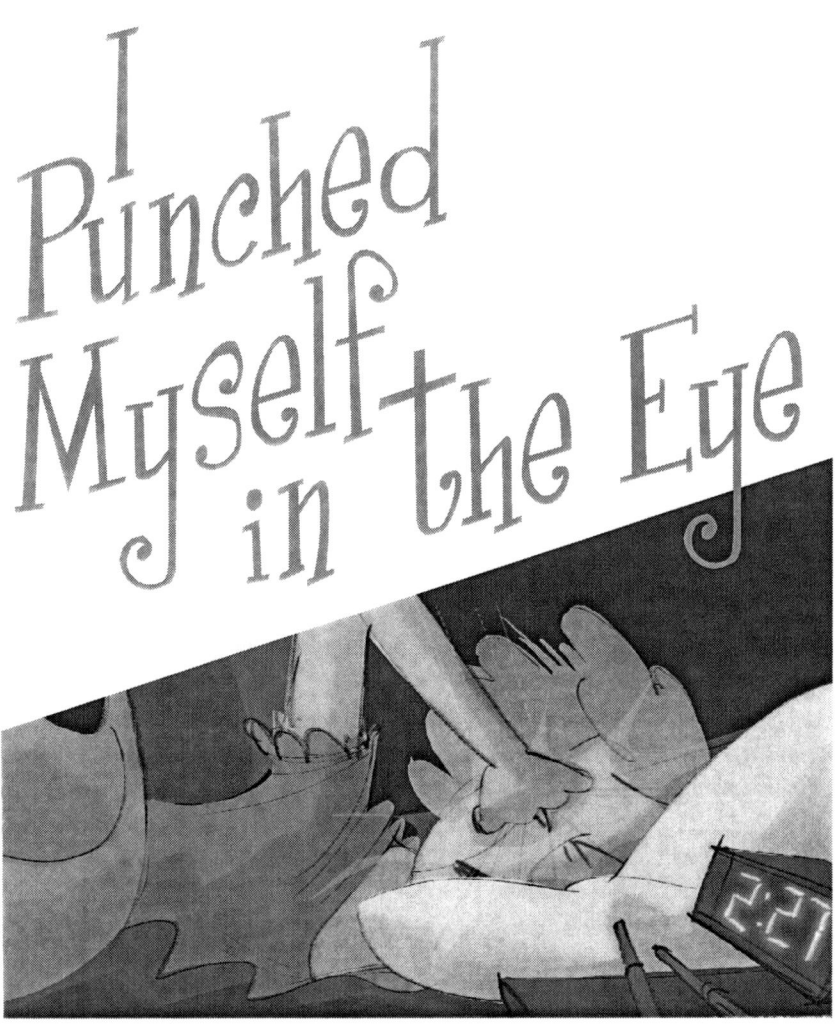

Stories of self-sabotage, imperfection and perfect, amazing grace

Pamela Capone

Copyright © 2015 Pamela Capone
PO Box 2422
Laguna Hills, CA 92654

eBook available at amazon.com.

Library of Congress Control Number: 2015918747

All rights reserved. No part of this publication may be reproduced, stored in a retrieval system, or transmitted in any form or by any means—electronic, mechanical, photocopy, recording, scanning, or other—except for brief quotations in critical reviews or articles, without the prior written permission of the copyright holder.

For foreign or subsidiary rights, contact copyright holder.

Cover design by graphic designer Tony DeCaro and artist Glenn Harmon. Interior art by Glenn Harmon.

Some names and identifying details have been changed to protect people's identities.

Published in association with The Wayne Hastings Company, LLC
Interior design and typesetting by Jeff Jansen | aestheticsoup.net

ISBN: 978-1519102102

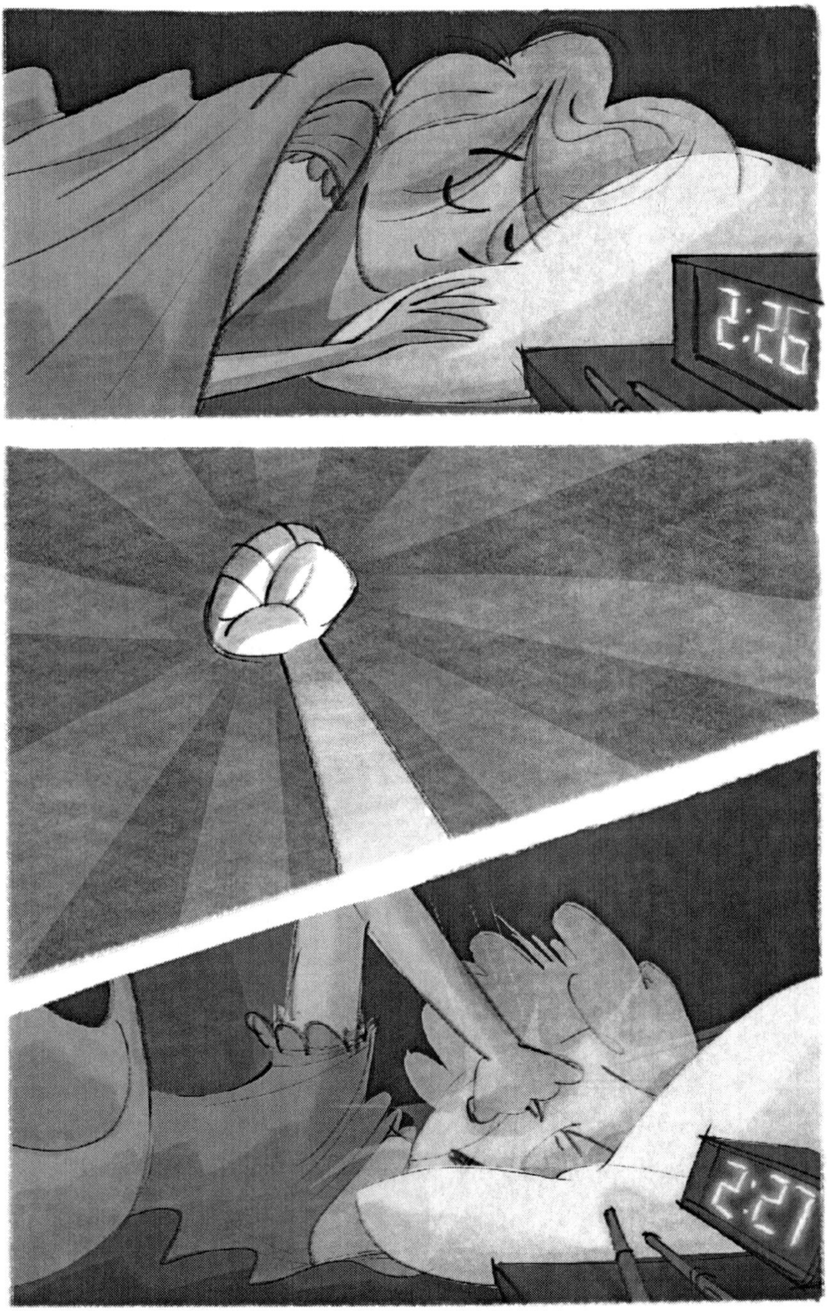

Illustration by Glenn Harmon

To Joe and Jean Ciarolla, who caught me as a babe.

To John Capone, who caught me as his babe.

To Joey Capone and Cassie Capone, the babes we caught.

Contents

Author's Note	1
Definition Page	2
Funny Dreams	3
Snief	5
City of Gold Lamé and Angels	8
Borders	10
Good Jean	16
Strong Man	19
The Fix	21
Parlez Vous Francais?	24
Going to Grandma's	29
Your Parents' Crimes	32
Resolve	34
Progressives	38
Insatiable	41
The Banana Thieves	43
The Sale Starts at NO	45
Gummy Worms	47
Fishy Guests	50
Rainbow Sandals	54
Lemonade-Stand Girl	57
Joie de Vivre	59
Even Babies!	62
The Day the Bread Went Awry	67
Pam on the Lam	72
Wish You Were Here	74
Conquistadors	76
Forgotten Identity	79
In Their Mothers' Eyes	81
Therein Lies the Rub	84
Pulp Friction	87
Garage Key	89
Fratello y Sorella	90

Up in Smoke	92
The Nerve	98
Night Train to Nice	100
Stolen Answers	106
The Exhortation Flatulation	109
The Crossover	111
THIS IS WHERE YOU ARE	114
Pinched	116
You Do the Math	120
The Bag	121
Can I Get a Witness?	123
Cart Before the Lord	126
Chapstick	129
The Intruder	132
Badpass	136
Brevity Levity	139
Hungry	142
Cup of Cold Water	143
Circles	145
Bijou under the Apple Tree	147
Budapest Ballast	149
Lab Work	153
Little Flower	156
Capri Diem	158
Little Miss Understood	160
Gold Dust	163
Emptying Nest	165
Button a Button	168
The Dash	171
I Love Lou	173
Is This Thing On?	176
Take the Cannoli	180
Pure Honey	186
The Mermaid Tale	189
REI	193
Bookend	196
Acknowledgments	198

Author's Note

This is a collection of non-linear essays, which means you are free to move about the cabin. Some friends and family were mentioned by name. I love an awful lot of people who were not mentioned, but that's no barometer of my love for them or their value in my life.

The story lands where the story lands. I'm just the catcher.

messay:

mess·y
adj. (mĕs′ē)

Informal, untidy, embarrassing, or difficult

es·say
n. (ĕs′ā′)

A short piece of writing on a particular subject, usually presenting the personal view of the author

Funny Dreams

I've been restless since I was a kid. Shutting down the little noggin has never been easy. The first time I heard Simon and Garfunkel sing "Hello darkness, my old friend," I was like *Hey, me too! I know that guy*!

The past few years, my sleeplessness has ratcheted up a few notches.

And then there are those strange happenings in the night. This particular morning after, I'd shuffled over to the bathroom sink and applied a squiggly line of Colgate onto my toothbrush, keeping my eyes 90 percent shut.

Opening an eye, I saw the other eye, which was black, as in, *shiner*. And then I had a flash of memory. Although I couldn't recall the dream, I remembered waking to the yowl and squeal of my own voice, my fist balled up as it left the scene of the crime: my own eye.

My more mature, slightly more alert, noggin engaged, I wondered: How often did this happen metaphorically? Without the benefit of conscious thought, how often do I self-sabotage, listen to that inner critic, become my own worst enemy, engage in mental gymnastics, worry about that which is not my business? Mostly, not let the Big Guy handle things.

Epiphanies never call ahead for a reservation.

There are other bright spots to my erratic sleep patterns.

Sometimes I wake up laughing after having had one of my more hilarious dreams. Really—the sound of my mirth will literally wake me up.

Sometimes the snorting and chortling will rouse John from his slumber and he'll ask, "What's so funny?" This is always of great benefit, because then I can recount the key points of the sitcom in my sleep, and we savor them—together. We're funny that way.

And wakefulness at night sometimes gives me proper time to work out life's kinks, piece together the puzzle, find meaning in the minutiae, maybe even embrace the grace I'd missed earlier that day—and pray.

Snief

Naked, covered by a thin sheet, I was in the zone. I love massage. I could get a massage every day and still be like, *Man, I need a massage.*

It was just the massage therapist and me in the room. Briefly after my bliss began, I heard a faint something creeping into my serenity. Tuning up the hearing on my ears, I lifted my head slightly. *What was that?* I wondered. The faint something got incrementally louder, a little rhythmic, then forced its way into the space like a jackhammer.

It was snoring. And the snoring wasn't coming from me. How could this be?

There was no denying it. My massage therapist had fallen asleep standing up. And yet she continued to massage me. No longer a deep tissue but a deep sleep.

She was a living, breathing, standing, snoring masseuse—the hired tired.

Did I mention she was snoring?

An unlikely story, sure. But it happened. I didn't wake her; I just let her rest. I figured she must be more tired than I was, poor thing.

Insomnia is a sneak and a thief—a snief. A snief in the night.

Sleeplessness exasperates me, leaving me completely beside myself. Truly, it's something like an out-of-body experience: I'll be next to myself in bed, trying not to disturb myself, only to wake myself further. I check the digital clock, careful not to shake the bed, and then I see that it's 2 am, and I completely lose my composure.

In a huff, I sit up in bed. "Do you see what's happening here? It's stupid-o'clock!"

I don't respond. I'm too tired. I just roll my eyes and turn over and give myself the back, like, "Talk to the back."

When you have sleep deprivation, you are highly distractible, crazy, forgetful. Wait . . . what was I saying?

The other day I had a bunch of dirty clothes wadded into a ball and was headed down to the garage to do some laundry. At the bottom of the stairs I took a detour and decided to go outside to get the mail. At the mailbox I retrieved the stack of mail and then put the dirty laundry into the mailbox. Thankfully, I came to my senses before I walked away. Can you imagine the postman's face when he'd open the box? I shudder to think.

There's an upside. Since you're half asleep all the time, you're generally pretty relaxed. And I've only fallen asleep while driving twice. Those raised dots on the yellow lines in the road sure come in handy.

Full disclosure: I get resentful that John can sleep like a baby—a baby at six months who sleeps through the night, *not* a newborn who nurses every two hours. John's the baby who falls asleep in the stroller in the middle of Grand Central Station at rush hour while a jazz drummer nearby wails away. He can saw timber with the best lumberjacks and not wake himself up. But when he complains about not having a good night (which means he rolled over once), I want to hurt him in ways a wife should not want to hurt her husband.

When he's especially nice, I look at him like, "What's that supposed to mean?" I was wearing an old t-shirt I purchased at Goodwill that says "McAwesome," and he made some sweet, off-handed remark about me being McAwesome, and then carelessly said, "I'm tired; I'm going to sleep." Can you wrap your brain around that? Do you know what I said to him as I sneered?

"McGloater."

My insomnia problem is not with falling asleep initially; it's with staying asleep. On a good night my internal obnoxious rooster crows at 3 am. That cockle doodler's like, "Rise and shine, lazy bones; it's five o'clock somewhere!"

Plus, I could sleep a lot better if I didn't have these darn arms to contend with. Sure, they're nice to have during the day, but while you sleep? Impractical at best; dangerous at worst. (See the previous chapter.)

Man, I need a massage.

City of Gold Lamé and Angels

Yesterday I was on my way to the gym and accidentally went to In & Out instead and ate a burger and fries. Weird, 'cause I totally had my gym bag in the car.

Some might call this undisciplined. Your lack of discipline might be my spontaneity.

I do some of my best overthinking on the road. Occasionally my head gets out of the way, heavenly light shines down, and the mental detour leads to Quality You Can Taste.

Today I was on the northbound Hollywood freeway, right after it transitions from the 5, in that little tunnel (underpass, whatever) where it curves and the pavement is completely jacked up. (We have no snow here, and pretty much constant, perfect, boring weather, so there's really no excuse, Caltrans.) If you're driving at high speeds through there, your car might need to be realigned afterward, or you might pop a tire, but if you're trying to blend a smoothie, you're in luck. So, it's actually kind of good to be inching along this patchy patch. Downside is if you're claustrophobic and start thinking about earthquakes . . . Try not to think *that* much.

Here's the thing about stopped traffic. You have time to see details, particularly when you come out of a darkened tunnel into the sunshine. You may be staring at gross trash, but it's details nonetheless. Like today, looking at the ground out my driver's side window, I perused multiple hubcaps, pieces of blown-out tires (likely from cars going high speeds in that patchy patch), standing beer bottles (they were going THAT slow), headlights with wires dangling, a strappy sandal, lots and lots of colorful broken glass, banged-up license plates, a full front bumper, AND a gold lamé gown!

Looking ahead, I saw the sky-scraping Bonaventure Hotel

where, thirty-two years ago, my husband John and I sat in the circular, rotating restaurant at the top, celebrating our day of engagement-ring shopping in the jewelry district below. Next, I noticed the unmistakable protruding architecture of the LA County Courthouse, site of some of my most horrifying childhood images—where my biological parents tried to take me away from my *real* parents. Beneath the courthouse are the murals on the freeway walls, paintings of children playing. Today the playing angels were free of graffiti, but I've often seen them marred.

If I could have craned my neck up and over LA's topography to view two miles to the east, I could see my birthplace, Los Angeles County General Hospital, now also known as USC Medical Center. This building is literally the face of *General Hospital*. I know, because I used to watch this soap with my mom. "Calling Dr. Brock Chandler Barrington, you're wanted in labor and delivery to usher another overthinker into the world."

I'm looking at the signature on my birth certificate right now and, true to doctor character, it is illegible. So that very well could have been the soap-opera name of his chiseled doctor self.

Anyway, that's where my story started, and I'm sticking with it.

As for the name *Los Angeles*, it is Spanish for "the angels." I was going slowly enough today through my hometown that I didn't miss them, the momentous buildings, or the gold lamé.

Borders

I was familiar with The Chicken Flight. Pollo Campero is Central America's answer to KFC, and many Guatemalans like to pick up a bucket when they're flying out. I loved my work with IMA, the girls' school in Guatemala City, so if breathing fried chicken fumes for five hours was the price I had to pay, so be it.

However, I detest window seats because of the penned-in, claustrophobic state. And on this flight, I was all cooped up. Officially trapped, I watched the other passengers board, many with chicken—a *cluck-cluck* here, a *cluck-cluck* there—earnestly praying my seat partner would be *sans* cluck.

As cluck would have it, a poultry-packing man sat down next to me. He too had gotten the memo about bringing chicken to the States, you know, in case chicken is completely sold out in America.

I could see the letters on his boarding pass. Trying to contain my excitement, I volunteered, "No, you see, you're in row *twenty-eight*. This is *twenty-three*." I enunciated in case he didn't speak English. "You must go back five rows," I offered as I pointed and sent him on his way. I do what I can.

A few minutes later, a couple found their seats next to me and began settling in. Deeply relieved that they were chicken-free, I acknowledged them with a welcoming, sleepy, grunt-smile. The older woman sat next to me in the center seat, the man on the aisle.

My brother and I used to draw a virtual line down the center of the back seat on long road trips. This would divide the territory and keep the peace. It was a clear boundary: Here you go; here I go. *Simple.* But even before we got out of the gate, there were bad signs on the horizon that this lady was not a heeder of that line.

She was clearly an *overlapper*. And to my thinking, she had no excuse. Albeit a little top-heavy, she had the small stature of a Guatemalan. I wanted to say, "Lady, have you ever heard the phrase *personal space*?"

What's more, right from the time she planted herself, she began rattling off run-on sentences. I smiled. I shook my head and said, "*No comprendo*." Who would keep speaking in a foreign language to someone who has just indicated they do not understand the language, and not only that, you're sitting next to someone on the other side who *does* speak the language?

This woman would. Let's call her Delfina.

The plane was not moving, not even a centimeter. And we were on a wing, so most of the view was blocked, and what was in view was pretty much nothing. Yet she leaned over me, her ample chest bumping me, fingers darting, motioning for me to look out.

I looked out. I smiled. I repeated, "*No comprendo*." I rested my head in my hand, leaning against the window and away from Delfina. I closed my eyes, perfectly executing what I knew about body language to indicate: 1) I am fiercely tired, 2) I do not speak Spanish, and 3) leave me alone.

Delfina did not speak body language.

The plane began inching along on the tarmac. The pilot announced—in English and in Spanish—that we would have a bit of a wait for our turn. So we waited.

Delfina continued to point. Delfina was *on* me.

This is when I began with the *I am going to have to hurt her* thoughts. Best-case scenario, I get no chance of having that arm rest. Worst case, I kill her in the sky.

Finally in the air, I began to strategize about how I could impart to her how it really would be in her best interest to back off.

I decided to play sick—speak the distinctive universal language of "I'm gonna puke. Maybe right on you, if you don't move away." I made gestures of the obvious nature, like holding my tummy and frantically looking through the seat pocket for a vomit bag.

When the sick act was clearly not making the impact I had hoped, I knew I'd need to take it to the next level. I considered elbowing her right back, you know, accidental-like. It could happen.

While I was busy plotting, she continued to speak at the man next to her (we will call him Edwardo) while still flailing her arms, wildly elbowing me, and pointing out the window.

With the plane now leveled out and our view still blocked by that stubborn wing, I wanted to yell, THERE'S *STILL* NOTHING TO LOOK AT! That's when I got the idea to look around and see if others had pulled down their shades. If so, certainly I was entitled to a little shade. I paid for this space, right?

When Delfina was deep in monologue with Edwardo, I reached up and pulled the delicate lip of the shade. Down. I felt exquisite satisfaction. For a moment. Then Delfina turned back to me, and to the now-closed window shade. I heard a distinct *"Hmmph."*

I thought, *That's what you get, Delfy. You wanna play hardball? Bring it.*

Undeterred, Delfina continued business-as-usual, minus the view.

About ten minutes after I had closed the shade, she met my eyes, smiled, and motioned that she'd like it up. I smiled back, nodded, and said, "No, we're going to keep it down." Delfina spun her head back around to Edwardo and barked a sentence. I wondered if she was telling him what a mean, spoiled American I was.

Starting to feel the slightest rumblings of guilt, I remembered flying alone once as a teenager and being seated next to an older woman. We hadn't spoken at all before I fell asleep. I awoke later to find my head on her shoulder, my mouth open with a smidgen of drool falling. I remember jerking my head up and quickly wiping my mouth. The lady just smiled and said sweetly, "That's okay, honey."

But this was not that lady. *That* lady was probably in heaven now. While we were *here*. Way lower.

I said "No, thank you" to the flight attendant who offered the fine United Airlines meal. Delfina was hungry. With her tray table down, fork in hand, and elbow out, the hounds of Hades were unleashed. I relinquished any attempt at reading my book, which I had been using alternately as border control and weapon. I found that if I wedged the hardcover book just so, in between my left thigh and the armrest, she would have a physical reminder like, *Hey, I guess maybe this is a line I just should not cross.* This worked slightly, but it also meant I'd have to give up on the idea of relaxing with my book and employ it full-time as a barricade. With Delfina and her devil elbows, it had come to that.

I looked at my watch. Not even two hours had passed. I couldn't believe how absurd this had gotten. I had been using the book to press against this woman and hold her back. Now I was increasingly brazen, moving my book back and forth a la Whack a Mole, blocking her blows, not caring that I was sometimes more in her space in an attempt to make a point: *See? How do you like it?*

This had gotten ugly, way out of control. I was deliberately hurting a senior citizen.

Realizing this, I shifted my thoughts to the IMA School in Guatemala City, where I had just spent the past week. Sixty or seventy years ago, Delfina probably looked a lot like the sweetest of the sweet girls. I pictured them in her face. I tried, anyway.

Just then, the flight attendants began handing out the US Customs and Declarations forms. As if someone had shouted, "Bomb!" Delfina and Edwardo shot up out of their seats in a mad panic to get to the overhead compartment. Elbows, rear-ends—everything was ratcheted up, and my few moments of reflection were out the shaded window as Delfina flung her backpack and another hard suitcase at me. Thank God for the quick reflexes I learned in grade-school dodgeball.

Surprising myself, I yelled, "Be careful!"

Delfina did not look my way. I was *persona non grata*. Edwardo was just as frenzied to get the passports out of whatever bag so they could complete the forms they would need *in the next hour or two*. I thought it could not get any worse.

I was mistaken.

When the coup de grâce came, all bets were off. Physically grabbing my seatmate by her shoulders, I pulled her toward me to meet my eyes and yelled, "You. Must. Stop. Bumping. Me!" Her jaw set, she looked away.

I was dead to her.

I felt the plane's descent begin, along with sweet relief. We were close to Los Angeles, and I would be rid of Delfina forever. I knew she'd want to see the landing and thought, *Honey, that shade ain't goin' nowhere! You're not seeing LA coming, and you're gonna be lucky if you make it to LA alive at all. Yeah, we're landing—and the shade is staying.*

Additional thoughts came rushing back: the lost man I had turned away during boarding, the hundred-dollar business-class upgrade I had turned down. I never knew I could descend so low on a plane.

I tried to quiet myself, to breathe, to pray. It occurred to me that maybe this was Delfina's first trip to the US. Maybe her first flight ever.

I thought about Delfina's culture, family, her personal space—and mine. Me, terrorized by a little old lady from Guatemala, who'd probably had her first airline food and thought it was *excellente*. She'd mopped up every drop of food on her plate.

Calmer, fed, forms filled out, Delfina rested her head back and I snuck a look at her face. I thought about the girls at the school I'd just left. I pulled the shade up, halfway.

Her eyes opened, and I heard a tiny "*Gracias.*"

I waited a moment and thought again. I pulled the shade up for full view, and we both looked out.

We landed at LAX. In Immigration, we had to go to separate lines—me to US Citizens, and her to Visitors.

I hoped she knew I was sorry.

I was.

www.imausa.org[1]

---

[1] Note: Because of the dynamic nature of the Internet, any web address or link contained in this book may no longer be valid.

Good Jean

When I compliment my mom on her youthful skin, she normally says something like, "I have good genes; I've got the Genaro skin." She doesn't deny the compliment (I mean, how could she?) but deflects it as a gift, part of her heritage. She also has a pretty snappy sense of style, and she knows that too, because she's been told quite a bit over the years. Some things you just accept.

When my dad had back surgery recently, I was on an extended stay with Mom at their home in northern California. I stayed with my mom at night, and chauffeured her back and forth to the hospital and then later to Dad's rehab, every day. A few times along the way, we'd see an animal along the highway, gone on to his heavenly reward—what some might refer to as *roadkill*. Every time, I'd hear my mom suck her teeth and then emit a soft, "Awwww, poor thing." It was sometimes a possum or another nasty rodent, and she'd react with that level of compassion as though it were a child's pet golden retriever.

When the rubber meets the roadkill, she's all about everyone else.

Jean Genaro Ciarolla is a character with character. When I was at her home, I had several duties. One was to answer the phone. Her instructions: Answer the phone, find out who it is, and then hang up.

She has the kind of caller ID that audibly announces the "intruder," and so most of the time she already knows it's a telemarketer, which she wants to avoid. Rather than letting it just go to the answering machine, though, she wanted me to physically pick up the phone and then hang up immediately.

My mom is a feisty one—stalwart, confident in her own way, direct, firm outer shell but soft, chewy center, heart of gold, true.

I've never seen anyone transform so dramatically when encountering someone in pain or need. One minute she's her cantankerous self, reciting an incident when she had to give someone the *whatfor*, and then a minute later, in a this-needs-empathy moment, she's as soft as a bowl of her perfectly whisked, mashed potatoes.

It was her idea—her split-second decision to take me home when, at eighteen months old, I didn't have one. She, along with my dad, swooped in and rescued me. Beginning and end of story.

Okay, so it's not the end of the story.

Let's talk about food. Here's an example. I don't know how she does it, but she has the ability to make a mundane iceberg lettuce salad taste better than the fancy schmancy field greens from the Waldorf Astoria. It doesn't make any sense. It's iceberg lettuce. It's supposed to be boring—that's its job. I don't know if it's the sliced radishes, the green onion, the diced tomatoes, the generic vinegar and olive oil, or the salt and pepper. It's barebones, and it's fantastic. Always hand-tossed, the only thing I can figure is that it's because it's her hands are doing the tossing.

As a little girl, I loved the comforting sound of my mom walking down the hallway at night and bending down to switch on the nightlight—that *click* of the light was my signal that she was about to tuck me in. I loved this moment. Once I was properly tucked, I knew that if I later got sick or had a bad dream, all I would have to do is call out to her and she'd be there instantly. She'd never make me feel guilty for waking her, and I never sensed she was annoyed by the interruption to her sleep. She knew I needed her.

I did. I do.

During my stay up north, we went to the home of some family friends one night for dinner. Someone said, "I know why you turned out so great, Pam; just take one look at your mom."

At church one Sunday, someone told my mom that we look

alike. I heard this a lot growing up, and I loved it. Jean Ciarolla didn't give birth to me, but in a way, she did.

Sitting side by side in church—the church John and I were married in—I recalled the days as a child when I sat with her and with my trusty little baggie of dry Cheerios, in case I'd get hungry. How, when I'd get sleepy, I'd lay my head on her lap and she would stroke the wispy hair on my temples. Hers was a touch of heaven.

If I know how to love, it's because she taught me how.

Technically, she was unable to pass her good genes onto me, but she did pass down her good Jean to me. She gave me her heart.

Strong Man

Age-wise, I was probably a single digit that day at the carnival with my dad. As we stood in line for the Hi-Striker, I watched each man give it a solid try, but at best the puck only shot up a third of the way. One by one, they'd all just sort of slink away. Vertically challenged, my dad walked up, grabbed the hammer, and in one wallop made that bell sing. A small grin appeared on his handsome face, and then a silent nod to me. "Let's go."

I was a goner with my dad. Still am. I'm still so impressed by his accomplishments, his underdog spirit, his fortitude. He has the kind of strength that I compare all other men by.

Oh, the stories:

He once chased a cow through a town. Cow gave up.
Caught himself on fire.
Almost shot himself with his own gun. Bullet came within a centimeter.
Inhaled poison.
After nearly drowning in a canal, he was saved by a young boy.
Fell off of a roof, flat onto his back. Walked away.

And these are just some of the things on his resume.

See, he had me at "Oh, okay." I don't know exactly what he said to my mom when she suggested they bring a foster child home. But I think "Oh, okay," was in the ballpark because I never heard that there was any debate. My mom saw a need, my dad agreed that I needed a home, and they had one.

This would come to be the way things worked for them. Someone needs help? *Oh, okay.* In both of them, the compassion gene is dialed in. He's the perfect companion for my mom, who has an amazing resume in her own right.

I have a distinct memory of my dad quietly saying, "I'll get the baby," and carrying fake-sleeping-me from the back seat of the car into the house. Miss that chance? Not me.

The embodiment of the American dream, Joe Ciarolla is the proudest humble man I've ever met. Self-made, and yet he'd be the first to say it's all been God's gift. He's street smart and unruffled by the letters behind someone's name. He's also true; if he said he's gonna do it, he will.

And he's an enigma. A traditional man by and large, yet with feminist qualities when it comes to my mom, who he considers an equal partner. He's also short and to the point, but a tall, winding storyteller. He still surprises me, but not really. Things fit, make sense. Almost predictable, but not quite.

Being able to call him "my dad" is what grace sounds like to me. It's unmerited favor, an unexpected gift. Miss this chance? Not me.

My first strong man—a man of steel with a heart of gold—he continues to pack a wallop. Until he makes that bell sing at the fairgrounds in heaven, I'll stand by his side. Awed.

The Fix

I was in a fix.

I loathe shopping malls, but last night I was between a nut and a chew, forced to go buy my own two-pound box of See's.

Can you imagine? John was out of town on a weeklong business trip. What was I to do? Wait until he gets back tomorrow night at, what, 10 pm, when the mall will be closed? That would mean, at the earliest, it would be Saturday morning before I would be able to sink my chompers into my made-to-order, chocolate-covered divinity.

I don't think so.

This time, John let me down. He let me down hard.

We have a near fail-safe operation here when it comes to me getting My Candy. The procedure is as follows: I keep my two-pound box in the top right dresser drawer and eat as I see fit. This way, I don't subject any other family members to the temptation of the 1) sugar (evil), 2) carbs (eviler), or fat (evilest). I am a wife and mother who loves. Deeply. So I certainly don't place others in harm's way by tempting them with the bad, bad things. I keep my candy out of view, *clearly* with others' best interest at heart. What can I say? It feels good to be a self-contained Neighborhood Watch.

When I finish the box, I gently and without fanfare remove the emptied white box with the contrasting black-and-gold lettering from my drawer and transfer it to John's underwear drawer. Simple. No big drama. No questions asked. The next time he reaches for his boxer briefs, he sees the box. I don't imagine that he opens the box anymore—that would be futile. He did in the beginning, of course, but no more. He just knows. It's time.

What I haven't disclosed to my supplier is that I give him a head start. You see, I have a strategy to prevent ever going without. And honestly, I want him to believe in The Urgency. Because sometimes there is an unfortunate lagtime (as has clearly been demonstrated this week). So when it's time to *pass the baton*, if you will, I routinely empty the box of my beloved chocolates when I am down to about half a layer (a two-pound box has two tiers, or layers), making sure to retain a safe amount in my drawer in a Zip-Loc baggie, tucked away behind my PJs. This gives me, in my estimation, a little breathing room.

However, this week we hit a snag. John said he had "a busy week at work." I just rolled my eyes and "telepathed" that his priorities were a little screwed up. If you ask me, he really just didn't make the time to make the See's run before he went to the airport on Sunday night.

He apologized as he left, but a lot of good an apology does when you've got an empty See's box. Of course, he didn't know about the baggie stash still in my drawer, and I opted to let his ignorance remain. After all, I have to think about the future and how this error on his part might shape how he plans for next time. Do I really want him to know there is a fall-back plan? I think not! Plus, I wasn't overly concerned. After he left for the airport with his apologies and luggage, I checked my Zip-Loc to see if I thought I had enough to tide me over until the new box arrives. I had my doubts, but still felt like it was possible if I rationed. Certainly in an emergency I could buy it myself; I mean, it's not like I can't drive. It's just that I detest the mall, and also, I just really don't want to steal my husband's pleasure in giving. I'm about the big picture.

A few days had passed since Sunday—and yesterday, I realized that I was tragically wrong. It was going to be difficult, if not impossible, to wait for my supplier. I would have to go. I would have to go to the mall. Myself.

And you know what? I did. And it was fine.

Now I have a near-full box wedged between my flannel jammies and my sweats. Perhaps I will hide them even a little better than normal and allow John the joy of buying me the box he so wanted to buy before he left. I remember how sad he looked. Why not allow him to do *this one tiny thing*? I can't think of a better welcome-home gift for him, really. It's the loving thing to do. Plus, two in the drawer is better than . . . well, you know the adage.

Will I speak of this ever? Unlikely. The way I see it, there are just so many downsides of that choice.

There are some who might see this as an unhealthy fixation. They say, "Hey, Pam, did ya get your fix?" To that I humbly chuckle. I'm not embarrassed by commitment. If I love something, I *really* love it. It takes me a good long time to get sick of something, and you know what? Sometimes I don't get tired of it. Not if it's good—if it's truly good.

Anyway, that's the way I See's it.

Parlez Vou Francais?

Yeah, I'd been around the block at Sunset and Vine. I'd seen a few things by now. No longer a newcomer to "the industry," it was my third commercial audition: a casting for a women's cosmetics line. My agent, Jerry, said I was to dress the part, of course—sophisticated, glamorous, powerful. *Check. Check. Check.*

Take-no-prisoners attitude. *Check.*

Characteristically punctual, I scanned the room, quickly sizing up the competition. No sweat. The performance had already begun.

I shot acknowledging nods at a few women—all dressed up, painted up, and presumably ready to step up. I knew that how one enters the room is as important as how one will exit. If how I arrived was any indication of how I would leave, clearly, I had this.

Exit strategy. *Check.*

Familiar with the drill, I took a casual look at the storyboard displayed on the wall. Sometimes this cartoon rendering at an audition indicates what I might expect behind the mysterious casting director's door. Unsure of the drawing's meaning this time, and seeing no other instructions with which to prepare, I assumed this one to be an improv. I signed in and then found an empty seat.

No big whoop. Piece-a pie. I'm good.

I considered my motivation. I was a savvy Hollywood actress, not to be confused with Pam Capone from Orange County on only her third audition. To busy myself with looking important (so much to juggle!), I pulled out my three-ring binder audition logbook from my briefcase—thick and filled with blank pages, I thumbed through and found page 3.

Audition: 3

Place: The Casting Studios, 5724 W 3rd. St., Suite 508, Los Angeles, CA

Casting Director: Hiroto Nakamura

Product: Cosmetics, Japanese commercial

My character and/or appropriate clothing: Sexy president and/or CEO of cosmetics corporation. High-powered executive, professional business attire, polished makeup.

Commercial to be shot in Japan.

Taking out a crisp headshot with attached blank resume and placing it on my lap, I settled in for further instruction. After ten minutes, an assistant to Mr. Nakamura emerged from behind the door. "Attention, people. Everyone who has just signed in, come on over and I will give you your direction."

Several upscale women gathered around the assistant. I hung back at the outer edges, tilting an ear toward the woman so that she would note my quiet confidence. This would speak volumes.

"You're coming in separately, but to save time, I will get you all in a group for the particulars. Now, you are a high-powered CEO. You're on the phone with so-and-so, and Mr. Nakamura will walk you through it from there. Got it?" Without waiting to see if we got it, she did an about-face and went to the sign-in sheet to read the first name in line.

Sounded easy enough.

When my name was called, I rose—demonstrating my energy, my enthusiasm, and all the while, balancing it with a bit of jaded flair. As I entered the casting director's office, I presumed standing before me was Mr. Nakamura, a very high-powered executive in his own right. I made direct eye contact, flashed my winning smile, and handed him my headshot. What I didn't extend was my hand to shake. That's simply not done at an audition. This I knew. Commercial Acting 101. What I did offer was a rhetorical "Hello, how are you?" as I made my way over to the masking tape *X* on the floor.

Directly behind Mr. Nakamura was a sleek mahogany boardroom table covered with food and drink, every seat filled with handsomely dressed Japanese executives. Eating and chatting, they glanced at me, and I again flashed my pearly whites. In return they gave me as Mr. Nakamura gave me: nothing. Not so much as a nod or a glint in an eye.

Off to the side and in the back of the room were big, black, foreboding cameras and camera operators—men and machines. They too looked blankly at me, not so much as a momentary look that might convey something like, *Hey, I'm with ya. I can see that this might be intimidating. You can do it*. Not that I really need that, but, you know, it would have been a nice gesture.

I knew this game; I'd played it. Twice. Pretty successfully.

"Slate your name, please."

"Hi, I'm Pamela Capone."

"Profile, please."

I turned to my right, still smiling my slightly aloof yet glad-to-be-there smile (striking that important balance), and then I paused, turned to my left, and faced forward again. Precision.

"Now, what I want you to do is pick up the phone and begin speaking to a subordinate," said Mr. Nakamura.. "Imagine that they are not giving you what you want and you are displeased. You are in control of your emotions and the situation, but you are the CEO of the company and you command respect. Yes, and I also want you to speak French. If you do not speak French, I want you to speak with a strong French accent. Do you understand? Can you do that?"

"Yes." *Oui.*

"Alright . . . Action!"

In my most assertive tone, I began: "Yes, er . . . *Oui*, I vant zose zocuments on my zesk no later zhan 5 pm, do you 'ear me? I am making myself clear? Zif I don't have zit, 'ere's going to be 'ell to pay. I don't care about zhat obstacle. Zhat is not my concern. We 'ave been through zhis before, no? I will not take no for . . ." and I continued droning on. And on. And on (with timely pauses allowing for my imaginary phone partner to respond), until Mr. Nakamura interjected.

"Yes, now while you are talking, I want you to notice a very attractive man in the hall . . . Keep talking . . . I want you to see this man passing by your door out of the corner of your eye, and I want you to make eye contact with him and seduce him with your eyes . . . Now I want you to use your body language to speak. Draw him to you, but keep talking to the person on the other end of the line . . ."

As Mr. Nakamura directed me, expecting me to comprehend what he was saying at the same time that I was speaking, I began to get flustered and could feel myself losing some of my French accent and the control I initially had over the scene.

"Now he is coming over to your desk, and I really want you to entice this man with your eyes. I want you to convey to him that you desperately desire him. You must have him now. Lure him with your eyes, your body, your aura."

I continued to speak—of what I was becoming increasingly unsure. I felt myself beginning to come apart at the seams of my Ann Taylor suit. I was unraveling before Hiroto Nakamura and his minions—cohorts, producers, the monstrous black cameras with blinking red lights. Something had changed. They were looking increasingly put off. I wanted to scream, "What? What?!"

And then I heard it. I heard the sound of my own voice, and I realized that I was no longer speaking with a French accent. My French accent had traveled many miles, in fact, oceans. I was speaking now with a very distinct, very strong Japanese accent—at the least a very Asian one.

Not good.

In what I can only describe as a dream-like state, I could see the little words—little, unstoppable plumes of word smoke—floating out of my mouth. I could hear the sound of my voice getting deeper and slower and a bit more garbled, like an old cassette player running out of battery. In the voice, I was still attempting to seduce a sexy invisible man by using a thick Japanese accent before an entire room of actual Japanese executives.

Japanese executives who wanted French.

And Hiroto Nakamura, casting director to the stars.

Trying to mask my own alarm, I looked at Mr. Nakamura, who was now silent. I scanned the room. No one was chewing. No one was speaking. Everyone's eyes burning into me, they were motionless. You could hear a blank resume drop.

I stopped, something a good actor never does until after the director says, "Cut!" or "Thank you," or "Please, just stop."

Mr. Nakamura was expressionless. "Thank you."

With a queasy smile I squeaked, "Thank you," and exited the casting room.

I closed the large door behind me, and as the knob clicked, I heard uproarious laughter from inside. Gathering myself, I turned back to the waiting room, gave a nod to the dapper woman seated near the door, waiting for her name to be called.

"Bleak a reg," I said as I strutted out into the sunshine.

Going to Grandma's

Sharing a room with my Italian-only-speaking grandma afforded me some special privileges.

I imagine my wide eyes the first and only time I saw her long, shimmery gray hair out of a bun that reached down to her culo (what our family mistakenly pronounced "cooley." We also called gnocchi "nockies"). Seeing her like that felt like an impossible treat. I thought, *Whoa, that's what was up in there all that time?*

Italians. Love me some Italians.

I am Italian. There is not one drop of Italian blood running through my veins. Still, I grew up in a home of four full-blooded Italians and eventually married an Italian man, so I think this qualifies me.

I stand by my Italian heritage. Digging through my mom's old photos, I came across a never-before-seen pic of my Grandma Josephine and me at five years old. I felt like I'd hit the grandmotherload—I treasure things that remind me of who I am: who I wanted to be, where I belong, and the gift given me.

Okay, granted, there are some technicalities on paper. I was the final child of nine born to two non-Italian starving artists in LA. And by "starving," I mean they sorta, accidentally, nearly starved their children—which is really not the best. Aaaanyway, at eighteen months, I was placed in a foster home, the Ciarolla home.

I lived with my new family in Los Angeles until I was five years old, and then just before I started kindergarten, we moved to the tiny town of Oakdale in northern California, where my parents had bought a vineyard. On those thirty acres was a small, old, broken-down home, a trailer, and space to build a new home.

Our family of five lived in the older home, and my grandma and grandpa lived in the trailer while my dad tended his new vineyard, built a construction business, and built our new home—all eventual successes. All of this with his own hands. All of this on a tenth-grade education.

After our new house was built, we got rid of the trailer and all lived in the new house, although my grandparents sometimes rotated living with other relatives. After my grandpa passed away, Grandma primarily stayed with us.

Peter and Josephine Genaro spoke not a word of English.

Sure, there was a big language barrier, but I did my share of gleaning. Grandma pronounced my name *Pelma*. I remember her always pinching my cheek way too hard while saying "*Bella*" (Beauty). My relationship with her was a silent movie with intermittent subtitles.

In 2009, John and I were on a trip to Italy to celebrate our twenty-fifth wedding anniversary. Taking a mostly unplanned detour off the beaten tourist path, we headed to Sulmona, a small town east of Rome. We had the name and number of one of my mom's cousins who lived in the town and could potentially, we were told, take us to see Grandma's Josephine's childhood home.

John and I debated whether we should take a day out of our precious Rome schedule. Mostly because of the distance to Sulmona but also because of the language barrier, since the relatives spoke no English. I mean, what could we do besides stare at each other and offer our Spanglish, or more accurately, our Span-Ital? Still, I had a hunch we should go, *carpe diem* and all that. So we drove a couple hours outside of Rome in the pouring rain, getting lost along the way, to meet Maria Angela and Ennio, our would-be tour guides to Grandma's.

Maria and Ennio communicated their warmth in spite of the

language differences. Every time Maria said "Mangia" combined with the live-or-die pleading look, I knew how desperately she wanted me to eat. I share this passion when I feed people too. I learned early on in my Italian life that this is the way love is cemented.

I savored the pizzelles like I hadn't eaten in days. I thought she might go into cardiac arrest once she understood that we couldn't stay for dinner. The shock on her face was both over-the-top and appreciated.

Our short drive over to Grandma's old place was fantastically entertaining. I love watching the way Italians interact, routinely yelling at one another like it's one of the five love languages—fingers jutting, arms waving, rolling down their windows as they pull their cars up side by side with their you-want-summa-this attitude. I found it quite impressive that Ennio was able to accomplish this in the two miles it took to get to our destination. The best thing is, after they're all fired up and have gotten up into each other's literal and figurative grill, they look at each other as though they're going to end with a respectful *Buon giorno* and a kiss on both cheeks.

Italians are fabulously forgiving people.

Holding our umbrellas in the rain, the four of us stood at the base of the home, long since abandoned. It was surrounded by weeds with deep roots. Looking up at the broken windows and chipped paint, I had a sense this would be well worth our time—more valuable to me than gazing at the Sistine Chapel. I had thought that going to see Grandma's house would connect me even more to my family, root me deeper. I was right.

So pardon me while I stand by my Italian heritage. Can't quite say that I've earned it. It was a gift. Much like the very best things—pizzelles, love, and life itself.

Your Parents' Crimes

Part of my morning routine is to check my email. Here's what was in today's inbox:

Subject line: "Instant Background Checks"

The first line of the email was a bold hyperlink: "Find out your parents' past crimes . . ." *Whoa.* Below that was a photograph of a little girl riding piggyback on her mother. Both were smiling warmly. Alongside the image was text that read: "Protect Yourself and Your Family. Use our online background check tool to find out if the people you trust are telling you the whole truth."

The people you trust.

Perfect.

They couldn't have known my story—that I spent my childhood and into my late twenties with that albatross of my parents' crimes riding piggyback. The sender of this junk mail couldn't know how well aware I was of my biological parents' failings and how attached I felt to them, unable to separate them—a loathsome symbiosis. I wonder, *If I clicked on that link and paid the inevitable fee, would it take me to the details of their stay in a Los Angeles jail, sent there for child neglect and abandonment?*

The junk mailers surely wouldn't know the follow-up story of the heroes who stepped in to serve as real mom and dad: Joe and Jean. It wouldn't have the details of the miracle in my life that removed the albatross from my back many years later, the miracle that helped me see Robert and Elsie Cole in a different light and forgive them.

Last year, I gathered with my relatives at the Cole family reunion in Texas, where I spent time with my biological siblings and their children and grandchildren. My sister Beth shared her extensive genealogy work, and through her we know more details. I was reminded of "crimes" committed by our biological parents, and by their parents before them, and so on. I was reminded of the complexity of being human, nature versus nurture, the tricky nature of it all, and remembered the Dorothy Law Nolte poem, "Children Learn What They Live."

My biological parents came from pretty broken places, and they lived what they learned. They had no tools.

That said, some pretty good stuff came through them. At my family reunion, I was reminded that my biological siblings are some of the kindest, most talented people I've ever met. You'd think they'd be bitter, but they're not. Which, I think, is pretty miraculous.

Yesterday I was talking to someone whose wife is expecting a baby. As we discussed parenting, I told him that I thought raising kids was the hardest thing I'd ever done, and that if I had to do it all over again, I would, though I'd do some things differently. As for my biological parents, even though they could technically be called *criminal*, somehow, I believe, they loved us. In their broken humanity, they did what they knew. But I wonder: If my children were to receive an email one day like the one that showed up in my inbox today, if they were to do a search on my "crimes," what would show up?

With the Internet, history can get current real fast. So I particularly like what David said. He was a pretty broken dude—a criminal, even—but also someone who, according to God himself, had a heart like his Maker's, and he wrote that when God takes away our sins, He casts them beyond the ends of the earth, where they are no longer remembered.

I think I'll print that one out. And delete this morning's email.

Resolve

Confused and groggy, thinking it was her normal 5:30 a.m. rise-and shine-time, my eighty-ish mom got up in the middle of the night and headed for the coffee pot tucked away in the corner of the kitchen counter. Battling a flu bug and likely a little delirious from fever, she did not quite make her destination. Instead, she lost her balance and fell in the hallway, hitting her head on the edge of a table.

Touching her temple and feeling the wetness on her fingertips, she eyed the blood dripping on the carpet and yelled, "Joe, get the Resolve!" Which he did.

My mom bounced back in a few days, carpet good as new.

I've had the opportunity to watch my parents love each other in sickness and in health, especially the past few years. For the first time, I saw what it looked like for them to be rattled that they might lose the other. It made me think of the Winnie the Pooh line about living to be a hundred minus one day, if Tigger lived to be a hundred, just so that Pooh would never have to go through life without his friend.

One of the ways my mom expresses her concern for those she loves is to stay current on what we might call *personal details*. Put another way, my mom is a bit on the obsessed side with *input and output*. This isn't just restricted to my dad. If she loves you, she wants to know what's happening in your intestinal tract.

She likes to keep track of your tract.

A couple of years ago, we'd just celebrated my dad's birthday at Red Lobster. In my family, special occasions call for special restaurants.

My mom and I were in the back seat of their late-model Buick, my dad at the wheel, and my husband riding shotgun. On a country road headed home to my folks' place, all was quiet. Then my mom turned to me, paused, and sweetly asked, "Did you move your bowels today?"

An involuntary guffaw erupted from deep inside me and subsided, only to return in another wave a few seconds later when I replayed the moment in my mind. I saw the concerned way she turned to me in the dark—when I thought she was going to say something meaningful—and I heard her ask me, tenderly, if I pooped today. I laughed out loud again, gathered myself . . . and the wave hit me again. And again.

My mom, smiling, said, "C'mon Pam, it wasn't that funny."

Yes, yes it was.

So, we discuss regularity regularly. Given that, it's understandable that it was her first question each morning when we'd arrive at my dad's rehab, while he was recovering from back surgery this past year—what with all the binding painkillers he'd been taking.

"Joe, did you poop during the night? Did you eat your dinner after I left?"

My dad loathed the rehab food. L.O.A.T.H.E.D. Do you blame him? He's used to my mom's cooking. All that yummy roughage.

My mom enters the room and begins shoveling food down his throat.

"Joe, c'mon. YOU HAVE TO EAT."

"Jean, I'm not hungry."

"Here, eat these peaches. You like peaches."

He rolls his eyes at me. My mom feeds my dad the peaches.

"That's enough; I don't want anymore to eat," he says, not quite convincing her.

"Okay, now let's have some Jell-O and maybe some of this cottage cheese. Oh, this turkey and gravy sure look good." (I saw it. Didn't look good.)

My dad scowls at my mom, gives me a can-you-save-me look, and then opens his birdie mouth as he sees the spoon closing in. It's coming, and there's not a lot he can do about it. Sure, he can clamp his mouth shut nice and tight, but he knows his wife: resolved, aka relentless.

Ironically, a few months before this, my mom was sick with a horrible case of the flu (a different time from the Resolve incident) and was dangerously dehydrated. The doctor looked her eyeball to eyeball and told her she could die if she didn't start drinking liquids. (We all told her this.)

She looked down at her feet. "It didn't taste good. It doesn't want to go down," was her standard response.

Water didn't taste good.

A few days later, I overheard my dad, kneeling by her bedside and with panic in his voice, sweetly begging Mom to drink and tearily praying for her.

I always knew my parents loved each other and had a good relationship. As I grew older, I began to suspect that they were perhaps the best representation of a loving marriage I had ever seen—a perfectly imperfect team. They had no rose-colored glasses, but they chose to look through eyes of love. Each equally respectful and reverent of their union but able to laugh at and with each other like nobody's business. Sixty-four resolved—some might call stubborn—years later, they still play and hold hands and have long chats in the morning over the kitchen-corner coffee pot. And they pray together.

Life has toughened and tenderized them. Since my dad's surgery and heart attack, he's broadened his horizons. One day when I called, he told me he was in the kitchen helping my mom bake a cake. He calls me on the phone and tells me "I love you," not like the old days of a rushed and muffled "We love you" after I said I loved him first. He's also much more chatty on the phone and often creeps into the conversation when I'm on with my mom. She and I will be talking for a while when he'll chime in, and I realize he's been on the extension all along, just listening, and then eventually giving his two cents.

"Oh, hey, Dad."

What's really hilarious is when he suddenly chimes in and then it evolves into a lengthy conversation between the two of them and I become the accidental creeper, listening in. No kidding, once they even debated about the specifics of his regularity. Finally, she yelled at him: "C'mon Joe, get off the phone and go outside!"

What I can say about my parents, and one of the reasons I respect them so much, is that wherever they have found themselves in life, they've had foresight, patience, stamina, selflessness, grace . . . and resolve. They didn't think twice about giving me a home when I needed one as a toddler. They just knew it was the right thing to do.

And being the big-picture seers that they are, I assume that, if one of them got confused along the way during all their years of marriage, the other was always there to say, "Get the resolve." Or just, "Go outside."

Progressives

A few years ago I started noticing the lines on the side of my mouth, cleverly coined as "a parenthesis." It's a thing. Stopping into a skin-care spa, I asked the front desk lady if they sold any good creams to help diminish these deeper lines. She looked at my face and, without hesitation—stone-cold serious—she replied: "You're going to need a plastic surgeon for that."

That was one of my earlier slaps in the face with aging.

When my daughter was a child, I had read *Reviving Ophelia: Saving the Selves of Adolescent Girls* by Mary Pipher. I was on board with the progressive philosophy. I railed against society's unrealistic ideas of beauty. I worked hard at saving my daughter's adolescent self, pointing her to better truths. This past week I had an offer to play a part in a short film. My role was that of an assisted-living resident. I said no thanks.

Within a couple of days I got an offer to do a wrinkle commercial for a dermatology clinic. I was told to wear no makeup on my video audition. Apparently, they felt my wrinkles were up to snuff, and I was offered the job. I thought about it and agreed to do it because I felt it might be a good exercise in acceptance. You know, dealing with "what is." My thought was, *Hey, life is just a series of seasons, and I may as well welcome this one, because what is the alternative, really? Do I want to be that cliché—the aging woman in denial, madly fighting against her mirror? No, I do not. This will be good for me. I'm getting older. So what? I'm progressing.*

A couple of days later I received the storyboard and my lines on my smartphone. The lines were absurd and humiliating, and it was everything I could do to fight the temptation to text the casting director and come up with an excuse for why I had to bail out.

The shoot was the next day though, and I just could not, in good conscience, leave the producers in a lurch.

But those lines:

"I woke up one morning, and I could not believe myself, how severe the wrinkles in my face were getting. I can't go out like this. I've got to do something about this."

And then:

"I called The Impeccable Skin Clinic, and I feel so refreshed! What are you waiting for? Make that call!"

The switching of tenses didn't make sense. Worse, the awful, underlying message was astonishingly clear. But I had made a commitment. So I memorized my lines and went to the shoot.

On shoot day, I was thrilled when the director didn't take one look at me and say, "Yeah, you've been perfectly cast. You've got more than enough wrinklage." It was reassuring to know they were going to "ugly me up" and apply heavy makeup to give me more wrinkles, age spots, dark under-eye circles, and bags. You know, for the "before" shot.

After I filmed the part of the commercial where I'm looking at myself in the morning mirror, completely aghast at my aging face, depressed and practically vomitus, I went back to makeup, to get beautified for the "after."

The shoot was on location, and there wasn't a mirror around, so I had no idea just how pretty they were making me, but the makeup artist sure was spending an awful lot of time on me. I could take that a couple of different ways: I was going to be fabulous—and happy about that—or super-sad that it was taking so long to make me pretty enough.

I chose to be positive and feel pretty. With cameras rolling, I raved about the miracles the Impeccable Skin Clinic performed and how my life had been transformed by having gone there . . .

The whole thing was ad-libbed or lines fed by the director. None of what I said was the original lines I memorized, but what I did say was equally as ridiculous. I'm sure even my tenses were screwed up. I hated every word coming out of my heavily made-up mouth.

After we wrapped, I got into my car to drive home, but not before looking into my rearview mirror. My mouth dropped. I was hideous!

Alone in my car, I yelled, "THIS IS THE AFTER?!" I could not believe this was what they were going for. I grabbed a tissue and wiped off the horrible, dark-black eyebrows, but the rest would have to wait until I got home, and then, of course, I would scrub all forty layers off my face.

Then I remembered that I had a stop to make at the optical store to get measured for what used to be called bifocals (old-people glasses), which are now referred to as "progressives." Sort of the way what used to be called used cars are now said to be "previously owned." I preferred going home first to wash my face but realized I might not make it before the store closed for the day, so I thought I'd once again get over myself and throw vanity to the wind, grow the heck on up.

When I walked in, the optician who'd helped me the week before did not recognize me. I was not surprised. I barely recognized myself in the rearview.

The next day I showed my twenty-six-year old activist, progressive daughter my iPhone video clip of me practicing my lines. Just so that we were clear, I reiterated that I was opposed to the message the commercial sent and all that, but well, I am an actress. Silently, I knew that I would not have chosen to do that commercial when she was an impressionable child. ". . . I was just doing my job," I continued.

To which she replied, "Yeah, just like the Nazis."

Insatiable

In Guatemala, there are several IMA students who live right outside the walls of the school. Every morning as I head up and down a hill for a little cardio before the day begins, I pass by these sweet, tiny IMA girls in their yard and we always greet one another with a *buenos dias*, a smooch, or an *I love you*.

Today, it got *loco*.

It was quite harmless when it started. Like any other day, they saw me and called me by name—but this time they said, "I love you, I love you." Twice. *Huh. That's how it's gonna be.*

So I said, "I love you, I love you, I love you." Then all heaven broke loose as we got competitive, trying to out-love each other. Picture it: me, sweating in the hot sun, huffin' it up the hill, yelling—screaming—"I love you, I love you, I love you!" Even as I crested the hill and we could no longer see one another, I heard the tiny voices trying to beat me. *Ha, I scoff at this.* The locals had been looking at me like I was nuts before today, watching me go up and down this hill. Now what must they think?

To keep things exciting, by the fourth time up, I incorporated different accents and voices which they, of course, mimicked—from operatic to baby and male voices, to quiet, sad, happy, and silly voices, to cowboy twang and sing-song voices—you name it.

By my eighth trip up the hill, we were adding groovy dance moves and anything else we could think of. Standing just outside their gate on the road, they copied everything I did, wildly giggling. Bonking ourselves in the head while saying I love you. Going cross-eyed saying I love you. Pulling on our ears saying I love you. Jumping jacks saying I love you. Walking backwards saying I love you. Rubbing our tummies saying I love you. A scene in *Garden State* comes to mind when Natalie Portman's character suggests to Zach Braff that they stand in one place and do crazy, odd movements and noises simply because no one had ever done that very thing in that very spot before.

On my tenth time down—which would've been my last anyway—it was quiet. No "I love you." As I approached their yard, I saw that the gate was now closed and the girls were quietly sitting and playing. Looking up at me, they smiled and whispered, "I love you." I think I got them into trouble. I guess we overdid it.

As I walked up the hill, I wondered how many times in my life I've tested God. How many times I was insatiable. How many times I've asked him to stand on his head saying I love you before I believed him.

He says it every day in many voices, places, and ways. Even when I can't see him, even when I've crested a hill, I doubt and think I have no evidence. Still, he just keeps saying it. *I love you, I love you, I love you.*

The Banana Thieves

One day while I was at the IMA Guatemala Girls School a few years back, I'd heard that a couple of little girls in street clothes had snuck through the open IMA gate and made their way to the holy of holies—the IMA kitchen—where they lifted some bananas. They were seen hightailing it back through the crack in the gate they'd snuck through. The girls were a bit of a blur, so the witness wasn't absolutely sure enough to ID them.

The next day, outside the gate, I was ambushed by two cutie pies so thick with dirt I could barely make out their eyes. I recognized them as IMA girls—one a current student and one a recent mini-dropout (we'll call her Maria). When I saw her, I remembered that I was told earlier on in the week that she chose not to come back to school this year. I was very sad about that. I didn't know why in her particular case, but I did know that, culturally, school for girls in Guatemala is the exception rather than the rule, which is why a girl graduating from IMA is no small feat. And why IMA needs to exist.

With her eager eyes and sweet voice, Maria said, "*Zapatos?*"

She must've gotten wind that shoes were handed out the day before at the school, most likely from her dusty compadre. I looked down at her tattered shoes, thought about how many shoes were left over and if we had a pair her size. I made the universal index finger gesture of "Wait a minute, I'll be right back."

Finding IMA staff, I asked them if we could make an exception for her and give her a pair. We all had the same looks on our faces, and I'm guessing the same inner turmoil. The American staff who were present were inclined to give her the shoes; the Guatemalan school principal offered wise insight: it would send a bad message, that she doesn't need to come to school but will still get this perk.

I thought, *Well, what about grace? What about THAT?* Unmerited favor, *ever hear of that?* And then I remembered that all I have to do is crack open Proverbs, where there is lots to say about working and getting. This is maybe one of those times that the old-school lesson is crucial. Ultimately, the consensus was that it probably would not be a good idea to give shoes to Maria.

Then I had a flash of hope: *Maybe this was all for the best. Maybe this was what was supposed to happen.*

I asked our principal if she would come down the hill and dangle the education carrot: Tell our little dropout that if she drops back in, she could have the kicks.

The principal agreed. She spoke to Maria in Spanish and then asked me if there was anything I wanted to say. With my wise translator, I told her that I loved her and wanted her to have not just a good pair of shoes but a good life, and that it's her choice. I wanted her to get an education so she can get a job and buy her own shoes. I pointed to the Asics I was wearing and told her that I got these nice shoes from working at a job (well, technically, John did). I told her if she'd come to school tomorrow, we'd have shoes waiting for her. I could see her wheels turning, but she was quiet. Before we walked away, she said she was going to talk to her mama. We waved *adios*.

Later, the witness who spotted the banana bandits confirmed that these two were, in fact, the same girls.

Three years have passed, and if all goes as hoped, this fall Maria's shoes will carry her across the platform to receive her sixth-grade diploma, just steps away from the holy of holies—and the bananas.

The Sale Starts at NO

The door-to-door sales were relentless, so I put up a sign on our door that says, "NO SOLICITING: We like our vacuum, we found God, and we gave at the office." This was never intended for Warren. Warren was my friend and my brother-in-law. Warren had a way of making me feel like he was the president of my fan club. Maybe he made everyone feel that way.

Warren sold meat and drove around in a refrigerated truck. I can't think of anything harder to sell door-to-door than meat. I can't even believe that's a thing. But Warren pulled it off, and he pulled it off so well that his business thrives, in part because of his tenacity in those early years of building his business with his wife, Cheryl.

A few days after I'd put up the sign, I came home and found the sign flipped over, and wedged into it was Warren's Dynamic Gourmet[2] business card. Warren was persistent. He later told me that when he saw a No Soliciting sign on someone's door, he saw it as more of an invitation. His exact words were "The sale starts at NO."

Warren changed my world for the better. I got him. He called me Map, *Pam* spelled backwards. We were both a little backwards.

Warren was simple yet complex, insecure yet confident, a wallflower and a walking party. He was a beautiful contradiction. Down to earth, yet with his head somewhere high above the clouds.

Warren had a friend who had a connection to an organization that donates shoes to the impoverished around the world. Warren wanted to get shoes for the IMA Girls School in Guatemala and said he'd pay the shipping, which would be the only cost. After I

---

2 www.dynamicgourmet.com

submitted the paperwork, I received confirmation from them that IMA would in fact qualify and receive shoes, but the number of shoes was fewer than the number of girls.

I told Warren, and he was heartbroken that some girls would be left out. It was unacceptable to him.

Sensing "The sale starts at NO" tone in his voice, I listened as he told me to tell them that he would pay for any additional shoes as well as shipping, but we needed all the girls covered. I lost count of how many times Warren called me and gave explicit, redundant instructions about what I should say to appeal to the organization. I wanted to say, "Okay, Warren, got it the first twenty-five times you told me." But I let him talk because I loved him and I recognized this annoying persistence in myself.

Not long after the shoe plans were in motion, Warren died suddenly of a brain aneurysm. He was fifty-one years old.

Warren passed on before the girls received the shoes, but 120 little girls got new footwear because of Warren's love, his persistence, and his and his wife's generosity. And one girl stayed in school because of those shoes (see the previous chapter).

I still have the No Soliciting sign on my door. Occasionally a solicitor bypasses the sign and knocks anyway. I can't help but respect that.

Gummy Worms

I was having a writing sesh, on my bed with my laptop, when I had a hankering for a little something to tide me over till dinner. So I grabbed a granola bar from the pantry—one of the few items salvaged before the bomb.

The pantry shelves were virtually bare now, with me having gone through and thrown away most everything after battling a couple of recent cycles of those pesky pantry moths. I had tossed out so much food, it made me sick to think of all that waste. Then I'd dropped some serious coin at The Container Store, revamped the whole cabinet, streamlined that sucker after setting off a couple of moth bombs. I showed 'em who's boss.

These surviving granola bars were now in an expensive, airtight container. There were no signs of moths or larvae with them, so I kept them.

Opening up the wrapper, I noticed how closely the flaky texture and color of the bar resembled the pantry moths—it would be virtually impossible to see a moth in there. I mean, as if there could be.

Pulling the bar apart, I relished how soft and fresh it was. *Boy, these containers sure are keeping these bars moist*, I thought. *So glad I made the investment. They're kind of gummy, even. Tasty.*

And then I saw the worms: the shimmying, squiggly, living, breathing, terrorizing worms.

In this order, I:

Screamed.

Spit out the contents of my mouth all over my bed and carpet. I didn't even care.

Threw out what was left of the granola bar.

Kept spitting on the floor and scraping my tongue with my fingers.

Ran to the bathroom, gargled, and rinsed out my mouth.

Checked my teeth for worms.

Brushed my teeth.

Flossed.

Drank a gallon of water.

Threw up.

Repeated these steps.

After I composed myself, I cleaned up the spit-up mess and sat back down on my bed, only to find another squiggly worm on the quilt. And then later that night, when I got into bed, a single worm lay in wait.

A couple days later, while in my car, I noticed one of those same granola bars I'd placed there a week or so before, just in case I'd get hungry while driving. I also remembered that there were originally two, and I'd already eaten one a few days before.

Here's the thing that wise philosopher Forrest Gump discerned: Life is a granola bar; you just never know what you're gonna get. Well, sometimes it's a wormy granola bar. In your tummy.

Forrest's philosophy applies to both the good and the bad surprises, of course. My favorite is when it's a good surprise, just to clarify.

There was a long stretch of wormy financial struggle John and I went through, and my hope of us ever owning a home again was dwindling. I just wanted to make a nest for our family and call it ours. I could identify with the first part of a proverb in the Bible that says: Delayed hope sickens the heart, but a dream realized brings life.

I had been waiting years for the second half of the sentence, but I was reluctantly accepting that it was not going to happen. I was a little heartsick. You might want to double-check with John, but my attitude may not have been the best. But then, without warning, a dream team came into our lives. It was one of the most loving, practical gifts of grace. It wasn't from a family member, and it wasn't as a result of asking these people for help. The dream fulfillment team essentially just said, "Hey, here's a fresh granola bar for you to enjoy. Don't spit it out."

And we've been savoring it ever since.

Fishy Guests

"Why don't you stay longer, like maybe a week?" I asked my sister Beth over the phone, after she was going over the details of her upcoming visit here to California.

"Nah. You know what Benjamin Franklin said about guests and fish stinking after three days."

There was no use arguing. She'd already booked the ticket from Salt Lake City to John Wayne Airport to celebrate her birthday at my house, and if three days was all I could get, three days it was. Although we talk regularly on the phone, the last time I had seen Beth was at our family reunion in Texas over a year ago. I missed her.

When I think of Beth, I think many good things—sweet-aroma qualities like patience, fortitude, stamina, commitment, resilience, love, laughter. . . and long legs. Like all of my siblings, Beth is a product of the California foster care system. She was in and out of foster homes and group homes, including MacLaren Hall in Los Angeles. It's been a hard-knock life for her. She even had eleven knee surgeries, primarily because she grew too fast—seven inches her senior year of high school—including four inches in two months.

She *had* to grow up fast. She's a survivor.

Beth arrived last Wednesday afternoon, the day before her birthday. That next morning, we were both getting ready for our fun birthday excursion. Our other sister, Ruth, who lives locally, was to meet us for a late breakfast at Lucca's, a mid-day matinee, maybe a walk on the beach, and then a sunset dinner in Laguna overlooking the Pacific, sharing a gigantic Texas Redfish between us three sisters—Ruth, Beth, and me. I'd bragged about the huge, deep-fried crispy fish. I was so excited about that dang fish, sharing it in the middle of the table like something out of the Bible.

Waiting for Beth to finish up her shower, I heard a crash and thud so horrendous, it sounded like a sumo wrestler had taken a tumble in my bathroom. Beth weighs even less than me, and I figured she'd either invited a small gathering of friends in there to bathe, or she'd fallen holding a metal file cabinet, a bowling ball, a cymbal, and a gong.

I ran to the door, "BETH! ARE YOU OKAY? DID YOU FALL?!"

She squeaked out a soft, "Yes."

I tried the knob. It was locked. "May I come in? Can you open the door?"

She whispered, "No," and then, "I'm okay, I think."

Several minutes later, she was able to open the door and hobble out, barely moving her lanky legs. "Maybe I can just walk it off. Let's go to the beach."

I saw the way she was moving—or not moving. This wasn't good.

"I don't know, Beth; maybe we should go to the urgent care. It's right up the street."

"Something doesn't feel right, like I'm out of alignment. Maybe we could go to a chiropractor."

"I don't think so. I think you need to see a regular doctor, not a chiro."

After a good bit of hemming and hawing, she agreed to go to the urgent care, where we met Ruth. We did that instead of the yummy breakfast, the matinee, the walk, the big fish dinner.

At urgent care, Beth had an X-ray that confirmed she had broken her hip. On her birthday.

She broke her hip. She'd need surgery.

I hadn't mentioned it earlier at the house, but as impossible as it seemed because of her youth, I actually had the thought that maybe she had broken her hip, because I had heard the disproportionate, impossibly sounding thud in the bathroom.

With her unfortunate diagnosis, we went almost straight to the emergency room at Mission Hospital. I say "almost straight" because it was not without a detour and considerable debate between us. She was convinced she needed to get back to Utah, like, *now*. Because she'd be out of her insurance network, the fear of medical bills was blinding. Ruth and I finally convinced her that what she was told at urgent care was true: because of the nature of her break and the main artery in her hip area, she was at great risk of a blood clot. She could literally die over this. She could NOT travel, and she'd need immediate care here.

Beth had surgery the next day, the day after her birthday. Surgery was a success, and by Saturday afternoon—the day she was supposed to fly back home to Utah—she was released and sent home with me and told that she absolutely, unequivocally could not fly for a minimum of two weeks.

She was not a happy camper. But she did what she had to do to survive. She walks things off.

Today marks one week since Beth's arrival to celebrate her birthday. Yesterday late afternoon, we were sitting on my couch, bonding like maybe never before. Moments too precious to share here. But before the touchy-feely, vulnerable good-love, I had asked her what she felt like for dinner—was she up for a steak, or maybe just leftovers? I mentioned I still had some of that yummy salmon from a few nights before, but I wasn't sure if it was still good. We counted on our fingers, *Let's see . . . one, two, three . . . yeah, maybe not. Three days was probably the max.*

As for Beth, she could never overstay her welcome. It's impossible.

If she's up for it, this weekend we'll head over to that oceanfront place in Laguna—just Ruth, Beth, the walker, and me—and we'll share a big Texas Redfish. Right after we say grace.

Rainbow Sandals

Saturday, 8:05 a.m. Groggy, I stretch.

I am bleary-eyed, have horrid breath, head of mop, when my sweet husband offers to get me coffee.

Handing me my joe, getting back into a warm bed, he asks, "Are you going out today?"

"No."

Thinking he may be wondering if today might be the day to take my car in for work (it's had perpetual warning lights, a door lock that won't work, etc.), I clarify, "Well, I don't have any plans to go out during the day, but I'm going to need my car to go to that comedy show tonight. Why?"

"Just wondered," he says.

"Are you thinking of taking my car in today?" (He had been asking me if he could take my car in for months now.)

"No, today would be the all-time worst day to do it."

Back in a far corner of my head, I knew this already, but was honestly confused. I knew John loathes to do anything on a Saturday that can be done on a weekday—you know, to avoid being a sheep following the herd—but maybe he was reconsidering his modus operandi. And if it were going to happen at all, we'd need to get on it, like, *right now*, before the rest of the sheep wake up.

"Yeah, I know. But maybe they're not busy today," I politely suggest. "I have had a lot going on during the week lately, and I'm having a hard time finding a time where I don't need my car for an entire day."

Silence.

More silence.

Little more silence.

And then more silence.

And then a low, steady hum just below the silence. I can hear the reluctant gears turning inside his handsome, sleepy head. He ekes out, "I'll give 'em a call and see if they're busy."

I remember him saying recently he's working on trying to be less selfish. And I'm what you call an opportunity-giver. I humbly agree, "Oh, okay."

He goes downstairs and phones our repair shop. I can hear John's side of the conversation, explaining about the warning lights and door lock, and I hear him say, "You guys are probably busy today . . ."

His voice is too low, and I can't get a sense of which direction the call takes. I conclude this is probably because he's sad.

Coming up the stairs, he says, "So, you wanna go now?"

Silence.

I'm thinking of suggesting that he take my car in on his own and schedule an Uber for the short ride back. I mean, it's such a short trip. What would it be, five bucks? And then I can stay in bed. It's early. And it's Saturday.

I decide against it and say, "Sure!"

Hopping out of bed, I put on my Rainbow sandals and get into my car and follow John's car up our street. We turn the corner and I see the most magnificent, full double rainbow on the horizon to the right. Leaving John's trail, I whip my car down a different direction, haphazardly park, and bail out, leaving the door wide open. I am standing in the center of a shiny street—mop head, bad breath, and clashing pajamas—clicking away on my iPhone camera.

A garage door goes up, and I see a woman in a wheelchair and her caregiver also gazing at the rainbow. We smile at one another, sharing this moment. Then I hear the distinctive sound of John's

Infiniti engine approaching. I look back and see him watching me, smiling. He sees the rainbow too.

We're all in awe of the glory in the sky.

Later, on the way home from the mechanic's, I'm sitting in the passenger seat of my husband's car and all is quiet. We turn the corner and see the same rainbow.

I break the silence: "You're welcome."

"For what?"

I point to the rainbow. "You'd have missed that if it weren't for me."

"That's true," he admits.

And it is.

Lemonade-Stand Girl

I make a habit of stopping at every lemonade stand I see. Sometimes, if I think I don't have time to stop and wave or give a thumbs-up, I end up making a U-turn and going back and saying, "Hand over the Dixie Cup, sweetheart."

I had been working on this book for a few months and had given myself what I considered to be a reasonable deadline. The deadline came and went, so I readjusted. Hey, there had been some unavoidable distractions and detours. *Not completely my fault*, I told myself. I thought I had made some good progress though, and I was curious how many pages I had written at that point. Using an online calculator, which converted my word count to pages, my eyes fell out of my head. I had thirty pages. I screamed, "I'M A PAMPHLET!"

That was not a good day. I did like the *Pam* in *pamphlet* part, so it wasn't all bad—lemons out of lemonade.

Before I'd begun my book a few months earlier, I had consulted a few authorities on writing and publishing. In a book published by a famous house, I detected some of the author's 'tude about self-publishing, which was a bit of flagrant snobbery if you ask me. No doubt, writers want to BE published. Who wouldn't want Random House on the spine of their labor of love? "Me, me, me . . . pick me!" I'm visualizing myself in the "yet to be picked" group at dodgeball, my grade-school skinny legs holding me up, all vulnerable. Not a fun place to be.

However, at the time of this writing, I'm not even planning to pursue traditional publishing. I might not know much, but from what I'm learning, it's making a whole lot of sense to self-publish these days, especially with everything so digital—books, music,

TV. Many films now are indie, and that's seen as cool, sort of boho. Times are changing. Though I don't deny that the Random House vouch engenders respect, we authopreneurs may not need The Man's seal of approval so much anymore in order to get our stuff out there.

What I think commands respect? The little girls who've set up a table at the corner, a poster board taped to the front, publishing in big, bold, red Marks-A-Lot letters, "FRESH LEMONADE," bravely and joyfully peddling their goodies. Atop the table, a pitcher of cloudy lemonade with floaters and some slightly burnt Toll House cookies. This is so impressive to me that I normally tip an amount that makes their jaws drop. When I say, "Keep the change," they almost always respond, "Are you sure?" and then, "Ohhhhhh, thank you!" as they quickly tuck it away.

You're welcome. We entrepreneurs have to stick together.

Joie de Vivre

Joie de vivre [(zhwah duh veev -ruh, veev)]:
A love of life. From the French, meaning "joy of living."

If you have a couple of kids, it's never fair to compare; to do so can only cause harm. They are individuals and should be respected as such. But canines and felines are altogether different beasts, and I have no problem noting the differences between the two. I'm trying hard not to play favorites. But I am trying and failing.

Walking into my daughter Cassie's dimly lit apartment and opening the dog crate, I am accosted by a two-year-old Jack Russell pup named Silas. He does the *shimmy-shimmy-shake* in his efforts to control his pure ebullience.

Tuesday the Cat is off in the corner with paws on the ottoman, gazing out the window at the lovers in the courtyard outside. Wearing a fuchsia beret, he looks over his shoulder as I enter, eyes dripping with condescension. He casually flicks his Gauloise cigarette into the ashtray, then looks back outside. Not so much as a meow.

While I was at the hospital with Cassie as she recovers from a couple of gnarly ankle surgeries, Tuesday had the run of the place, languidly sauntering about. Silas had been in his crate all day. For good reason, he is often called The Troublemaker. Though not by me.

Cassie had taken a nasty fall from a rock-climbing wall. Ankle ended up at an unfortunate angle. So I'm here in Portland on extended stay, hanging out. There's no place I'd rather be.

If Silas and Tuesday were in a boxing ring, it's safe to say they would be fit opponents, with less than a pound difference between them. They are like black and white.

While he means no harm, Silas is the master of the *coups de main*–what the French call a surprise attack. Tuesday will recoil and hiss. Personally, I think the hiss is scary. Even from a distance. But for Silas, he's like, *Whatevs*. He thinks it's playtime.

He's the consummate life-of-the party, and yet so much more. I know I'm at risk of sounding like a Paris Hilton-type who carries her lapdog in her purse, and I don't care. Silas is a tiny person in a scruffy dog suit. Just this morning I was making cooing noises in his face and Cassie said, "You know he's not a baby, right, Mom?"

Sure, I know.

I didn't think he could be sweeter or more vulnerable until I gave him a bath the other day and saw him all drenched and soapy.

Although I'm not the kind of person who can sleep with a dog, I wasn't judgmental about others who did engage in that behavior. Much. But now that I am sleeping on an air mattress on Cassie's apartment floor and don't have a choice? Well, let's just say, I've adapted. Silas's favorite sleeping position is directly on top of me. Second choice is spooning, and third is balling himself up in the bend of my knees when I'm on my side. His little snores? Ridiculously cute.

When I go home, I'm not sure if I'll be able to sleep without him.

He is a walking around on all fours, a thirteen-pound heart in his chest, an expert at both generously giving and unashamedly receiving love. If we humans could pull off that kind of love? There'd be no meanness to report on the twenty-four-hour news channels.

When Silas was at my home in California three weeks ago, I was horrified when he got into some unknown rat poison in the garage. Cassie and I rushed him to the nearest and most expensive emergency vet. I was traumatized.

On a scratch test at my allergist's office years ago, it showed that I am equally allergic to both cats and dogs. I've never had a real-life reaction to a dog. Cats are another story.

If Silas is a brilliant illustration of *joie de vivre*, of "Hey, I'm here, let's do this thing"–living and loving unabashedly with a Gumby-like, malleable, tender, trusting spirit—Tuesday represents the superior, self-contained, elusive, take-you-or-leave-you type.

Or does he? Maybe Tuesday is wearing an aloof cat suit.

Rather than the master of the *coups de main*, perhaps Silas is the master of relationships. And there's a method to his gladness.

Even Babies!

The grainy, originally-VHS-now-converted-to-digital video opens on the sound of a steady whine in the unfenced greenbelt "back yard" of our Laguna Hills condo. Watching my babies, I was the videographer that day in the summer of 1990, capturing three children in a small, round, inflatable pool. In the foreground is my baby girl, Cassie, a little over a year old who stays planted in the same spot the entire time, whine-crying. The two behind her are four-year-olds Joey and Robin. Joey's my firstborn, and Robin is the granddaughter of a neighbor who lived a couple doors down. Robin was around sometimes because her grandma babysat her while her mom worked.

I do nothing but observe and record.

Joey, to Robin: "What?"

Robin: "How come you talk so louder?"

Joey: "Uh-cause" [meaning "because"].

Robin baptizes Joey with water from her bucket. She looks over at me to see what I might do. Deflecting the water, Joey stands tall, straightens his swim trunks, pulling the hem down, making sure all is kosher.

Joey: "Uh-cause. Uh-cause I'm a boy."

Robin takes a drink of water from the baptismal vessel (the bucket). She beats her chest a la Tarzan's Jane: "I am girl!"

Joey, with a pointing finger and condescending, parental tone: "That's the way God made you." He folds his arms and repeats the sentence. "That's the way God made you."

Robin stands up, picks her bathing suit out from her bum, and asks, "Why?" Cassie stops whining for a moment and turns to see this new development behind her. She senses things may have taken a turn.

Joey, not really answering her question: "That's the way God made you."

Robin, clearly in utter disbelief: "He didn't make me."

Joey can barely believe the audacity. He's never heard anything so absurd in his entire life: "Nuh uh, yes He did! He made you!"

Robin: "No!"

Tempers are flaring. Joey gets in Robin's face, pointing directly at her, and then with his hands on his hips: "He made me and He made you!"

Robin is now screaming, her atheism and humanism fully revealed: "I made myself!"

Joey's faith is challenged: "Nuh uh! God made you and He made me."

Things deteriorate as Robin turns physical, hitting and pushing with an interesting pinchy-pokey maneuver using her claw-like hands while Joey desperately tries to resist hitting back. He maintains some semblance of decorum through a clever/awkward arched back, arms at his side, chest-bump/wiggle technique. He's been taught to not hit girls. With Robin's arms wrapped around Joey, it begins to look very much like the Argentine Tango.

Joey, still valiantly resisting Robin's assault, uses his words only and repeats himself to make sure she's getting the message good and clear: "He made you and He made me. He made you and He made me. He made you and He made me."

They both turn to a sudden, authoritative voice in the distance—that of Robin's Eastern Bloc grandmother. Robin relents and they both sit back down into the wading pool. Robin pulls a deceptive move and acts as though she's been trying to comfort Cassie, who continues to whine. Cassie isn't so easily fooled. She's well aware she's been ignored the whole time. Still holding the camera, I am riveted.

Joey, unwilling to give up the fight, but at a slightly lower volume, moves back into Robin's personal space and repeats his original declaration: "God made you and God made me."

Robin is 0-60. She once again beats her chest: "NO! I MADE MYSELF!"

Joey employs a sassy, *nanny nanny boo boo* tone: "Nuh uh, you don't know how!"

Robin is silenced while Joey takes the podium for his filibuster, but she deluges him with water the entire time.

Joey, balls to the wall (relax; look up the definition) and using his arms in a repetitive and embarrassing bird-flapping motion, says: "God made you and He made me and He made Cassie [points to his still-whining sister], and He made Mommy [points to me] and He made your mommy and He made your grandma and He made everybody! He EVEN made EVERYBODY. He made everybody. He made everybody. He made ev— [he wipes his eyes after another face full of water] . . .everybody! EVEN BABIES! He makes EVERYONE!!"

That about covers it, I'd say.

He looks at me, completely spent. I can see the hurt in his eyes. All but for tiny splashes and sweet gibberish from Cassie, there is silence.

He blows air through his lips, making the exasperated motorboat sound, shakes his head with an "I've done all I can do here" face, and turns his back to Robin. Lying on his tummy in the now emotionally heated pool water, Joey rests his face in his hands.

Cassie resumes a minimal-effort whine while playing with her pool toys. Finally, Joey catches a glimpse of his shriveled fingers and breaks the tension with an exciting new subject.

Joey: "My hands are like . . . my fingers are like raisins!"

Robin douses him with her bucket. She says nothing, she's so over it.

Joey, as though this were a direct affront to his opinion about his raisin-y hands, readies again to battle wits: "They're like raisins! NO! They're like raisins!"

The video ends.

I love Robin's early, earnest question, "Why?" You have to respect it. It's a question for the ages, and for all ages, even babies. Although I'm not exactly clear whether Robin was asking why God made her, or why God made her a girl, or whether He made her at all. I'm leaning toward the idea that maybe she was saying, "Huh? Come again? What do you mean, God made me? Who is this God?"

Meanwhile, Joey kept stating his supposition—simply, that God made her. He thought that should suffice. When she had a moment to think about what he was saying, Robin reacted as though it was the most obscene and ridiculous assertion anyone ever made. It's interesting how quickly and organically she made the leap to say she made herself.

We all make leaps. We leap into the direction of our own choice, whichever direction makes the most sense. Every leap is faith, whether it's to believe or not to believe. Not believing is still believing something.

I think there are many ways to share one's faith. While I tend toward the more subtle approach, we all have our way. Joey's impassioned way is one. To his very core, he believed what he professed, and to suggest otherwise was, until that day in the pool, unimaginable to him. Blasphemous.

There are aggressive, in-your-face "Bible thumpers," and there are those who believe: "Preach the gospel at all times, and if necessary, use words" as an out to speaking up. Some people believe it is a wise admonition to refrain from using our voices in sharing our faith—we ought to show rather than tell, because words are inferior to actions.

What I find in Scripture is the apostle Peter himself saying we should always be ready to offer an answer to anyone who asks about our faith, but to do so humbly. So personally, as a Christian, I think we are commissioned to employ both words and actions. Our talk must be backed up by our walk, even when our gait is imperfect.

We live in a tricky cultural climate. I get shy sometimes because of personal insecurity, afraid that I might offend and be a deterrent to someone coming to faith. I don't want to clobber anyone. I'm still working out my way, trying to do better.

When things get dicey in our respective back yard inflatable pools, we can hit, poke, do the Argentine Tango. We can change the subject, splash someone in the eyes, dump an entire bucket of water over our opponent's head. Or we can admit we don't have all the answers, and as we have seen come from the mouths of even babies, we can do our best to answer "Why?"

The Day the Bread Went Awry

This is not about rye bread because I *hate* rye bread; let's just get that off the table. This is about white, Italian, soft on the inside, crusty on the outside, yummy hot dough baked to perfection.

One of the first things you do when you make homemade bread is to check the key ingredient—yeast—to be certain it is active, ready to do the job. I mean, yeast is EVERYTHING.

One day, as I prepared to make a batch, I could tell after the first ten minutes that the yeast was bad. But instead of admitting yeast defeat (or as I call it, *yefeat*) and going to the store to buy new, active yeast, I stayed put and hoped that—even though the yeast failed the early test—somehow, some way, it would still rise to the occasion.

"It doesn't look good, Mom. I think the yeast is bad."

I convinced myself and my mom that we ought to still use it, add the ten-pound bag of flour along with all the other ingredients, and give it a go. I would knead that beast into submission.

I worked the massive wad into a roundish shape and put it into a slightly warmed oven perfect for rising. In complete denial, I suggested, "Let's give it time and just keep watch."

Twenty minutes later, the dough was not budging.

An hour later, it should have doubled. If anything, it got more defiant and shrunk.

It was time to either throw it away or just go ahead and divvy it into loaves and rolls and maybe a focaccia for a "second" rising, and then bake those suckers as is. Opting for the latter, I said, "Remember the Bible story about the fishes and loaves and how Jesus prayed and they multiplied? Let's do that." My mom smiled a faithless smile.

I've been regularly making bread my entire adult life and could only recall having had it go sideways once, and that was due to an unfortunate translation problem with a Guatemalan oven. I was teaching the IMA high school students how to bake bread, or in that case, how not to bake bread.

Now this time, it was in front of my mom. *My mom.* Who'd requested my bread. I'd been at my folks' place while my dad had back surgery, and early on in my three-and-a-half week stay, Mom had mentioned that maybe I could make a batch before I left town. I'd be leaving the day after tomorrow, and now was perfect.

This devil-batch yielded half the amount, The rolls came out like the hard balls that big-league pitchers use, and the baguettes could put an eye out. I tried to cut into one, and I needed a hacksaw. I put my tongue to it and couldn't even bite into it.

"Mom, I'll do it again. I'll go to the store, get all the ingredients, and make you a batch. I have one more day."

She wouldn't hear of it.

Some of my stubbornness is genetic, some of it is a learned coping mechanism; but a good bit comes from this woman. So I didn't argue. No point.

I came home and knew I had a week to accomplish all the Unpack and Repack for my next trip, which was to Guatemala. It was going to be a full week with not a lot of extra time, if any. Clearly not a day to make bread. That would be CRAY-ZEE.

Nearing the end of my week at home, just for fun, I stopped off at a nearby mail-packaging place to ask, hypothetically, what it would cost to overnight a box to Oakdale. I mean, if I did have time to do it, would it be feasible? Or would it just be nuts? That morning, John had mentioned the nice lady who is owner/operator of the local mailboxes and mail service. He said she's a full-on authority on which shipper is cheapest and fastest—USPO, FedEx,

UPS, DHL, etc. If I was going to get my mom her bread, it would have to be an overnighter or, at the very most, two-day, and it sounded like this lady would have the straightest scoop.

I told—let's call her Sadhana—my situation. I told her I made the bread with my mom, and the yeast failed, and I wanted to make her some again and ship it to her quickly, but I didn't have a lot of time and I didn't want to spend a ridiculous amount of money. Her piercing eyes filled almost immediately, and she urged, "OH, YOU MUST DO IT." In her beautiful, thick Indian accent, she went on: "My mother is in India, and she is very ill, and I can't be there with her, and I am so sad. You must do this for your mother because you don't know if you will have tomorrow. Don't let any moments pass you by."

In not so many words, I said, "Are you kidding me? I'm all about *carpe diem*. I have the tattoo! It's my thing! But you don't understand. I leave for Guatemala in two days. I have to pack. I have things to do. I just got home from being gone for three-and-a-half weeks, and I'm leaving again. In. Two. Days. Things. To. Do."

"Have you made it yet?"

"No," I replied. "And it takes three hours from start to finish." (That wasn't even allowing for any cooling time or packing and shipping and driving back and forth nonsense.)

"If you can be back here by 4, we can do it," she reasoned. Sadhana didn't seem to be hearing me.

I looked at the clock; it was high noon.

She nodded her head, "YOU MUST DO IT. I will help you."

I wanted to say, "DON'T THROW DOWN THIS GAUNTLET." Instead I said, "I don't have time to." Meanwhile, in my head I heard Clint Eastwood's scowly, growly "Make my day" and "Get off my lawn" voice: "You don't have time NOT to."

Ignoring the misnomer about not ending a sentence with a

preposition, I considered her proposition. One that I knew: We always say, there's always tomorrow. That's generally true . . . except on your last day.

Don't let any moments pass you by.

Sadhana elaborated about her dying mother, and I told her about my time with my parents the past few weeks, my dad's surgery, and his recovery. She said she would pray for my dad. I asked her mother's name and I said I would pray for her mom too.

She pled her case, "We can make it work. I will help you."

"But I . . ."

She put her hand up, smiled and nodded.

I continued, "I have to pack. I can do it when I come back from Guatemala. I'll only be gone a week and then we can do this."

"Oh, okay." Her eyes went dark, like someone pulled the shade on the window to her heart.

I live less than two miles from her store, and by the time I pulled into my garage, I put myself into sixth gear and kicked some bread butt. This time I really did pray. I also added extra yeast (okay, a lot of extra yeast).

I was back at her shop by 2:45 pm, armed with a large basket of hot bread and some wrapping equipment. Still too hot to wrap at home, every minute counted, so I drove/sped while steam hovered. Plus, she said she'd help me.

I lost track of how many times Sadhana came from around the counter. Hugging and crying, crying and hugging—all that stranger/human connection thing is so underrated. That's why we're here.

She saw that there were some additional, unpacked loaves, rolls, and an Indian naan flatbread, aka focaccia. "There is still room in the box, and it won't cost you anything more. We can fit more."

I told her that these were for her.

Back around the counter she came.

She mailed my package at her cost, and on top of that, she gave me a donation for IMA.

It's not always a given that you have functional, healthy yeast. Note to self: Believe the results of the yeast test. Sometimes a do-over is necessary.

Who'd have known my experience with a little inedible, unleavened bread would have yielded a friend? And who'd have known how much foccacia and naan are basically one and the same? Like Sadhana and me.

Pam on the Lam

From the IMA School in Guatemala City, Antigua is a half hour drive and truly a little gem—a relatively safe city compared to anywhere else in the country. When I visit the school, I always take a detour to Antigua.

My travel partner, Deby, and I were enjoying a wonderful Saturday. Indigenous people and tourists alike populate this city of ruins, lush greenery, and bright-colored colonial architecture. As we were meandering through the crowds in an open market, Deby looked at trinkets as I mostly people-watched, soaking in the culture.

Remembering that Deby didn't have her cellphone with her, I suggested we meet back at the hotel *if* by some chance we were to get separated. Good deal; no problem, she said. We'd try to keep ourselves together, but you know, things happen.

Moments later, I looked down and noticed a weathered old man sitting on the edge of the rickety boardwalk. On the other end of his outstretched arm he was angling a mirror. In that mirror's reflection I saw the underside of an indigenous woman's skirt. I wagged my finger in his face: "Hey! No! No! Bad! Bad!" The woman pulled away, giving him the stink eye and muttering something in Spanish.

Deby, apparently still in earshot, asked me what was wrong. "That dirty old man is looking up skirts with a mirror!"

She uttered a groan of disgust and then a sudden proclamation, "Well, let's go kick him!"

More than a little surprised by her idea, but without missing a beat, I agreed something more needed to be done. Unsure what that might be, we hovered behind him for a moment. I realized he was oblivious to our presence, and I saw a perfect opportunity and snagged the mirror right out of his filthy hand. I saw the fire in his eyes as I grabbed the mirror and pivoted. Reaching and swinging at me as he struggled to stand, I said nothing to Deby, nothing to the old man—and hightailed it across the cobblestone street. I saw the *policia*, and it occurred to me that perhaps I should tell them, but that idea was overruled by four immediate concerns:

1) The *policia* were corrupt.
2) The *policia* were corrupt with very large guns.
3) I was a woman in a terribly misogynistic culture.
4) I was a woman in a terribly misogynistic culture who could speak virtually no Spanish to corrupt *policia* with very large guns.

So, mirror in hand, I decided to keep running. I ran until I was certain the man and the *policia* were nowhere in sight and I could dispose of the mirror.

Deby told me that after I bolted, she saw the old man reporting me to the authorities, pointing in the direction I had fled, indignant, apparently urging them to come after me because I'd stolen his mirror.

When the weekend was over, Deby and I headed back to the IMA School. I thought of the girls. I thought of myself as a little girl . . . and I thought of that wiry little Antigua man. Could my face be on a wanted poster in a Guatemalan post office? It's possible. Would I do it again? No doubt. I went from people watcher to international fugitive. Sometimes when you and your friend shop for trinkets, you get more than you bargained for.

Wish You Were Here

Beating sunrise, John and I scurried like rats under the concrete earth into the New York City subway system. Eager to begin our Manhattan adventures, there was no one else on the ghost town platform. No one else, that is, except the subway musician, positioned near a wall, setting up his electric guitar and amplifier and tip jar. He seemed to be starting his day too. *Impressive*, I thought. *Ambitious.*

Then he began to play.

As I waited for the train, I didn't recognize the long instrumental preamble but was mesmerized by his pure talent, the exceptional quality filling my ears. I thought, *Go put something in that tip jar before the train arrives. Reward that talent.* But then his guitar strap failed and the guitar fell. His fingers now fumbling with the strap, he was no longer strumming the guitar.

Like magic, the music continued. The beautiful, professional-sounding instrumental didn't miss a beat, even as he did. Making eye contact with me as he resumed his strumming, the guy knew I knew his secret.

Next, he began to sing. Or should I say, the vocals began. He mouthed the words with feeling, as though he meant every syllable.

Maybe he did.

Appalled, I told John, who had his attention elsewhere and was unaware of the scam taking place. Turning his ear to the musician, he said, "Yeah, that's Pink Floyd, 'Wish You Were Here.'"

John is a Pink Floyd authority; this much I knew. I instantly recalled seeing the Pink Floyd posters on his teenage bedroom wall.

I thought I could tell raw talent from pure scam, but I was tricked. I was disappointed when I realized this "musician" was a shyster. All judgy, I felt betrayed and wished *he was there*, truly performing.

At the end of the day, on a different platform in a different subway station, we saw the same guy, performing the same song. Waiting for our train, the song came to an end and we boarded and stood in our spot inside, near the door. A moment after hearing the "Stand clear of the closing doors" recording, we heard "Wish You Were Here" begin again.

It was a continuous loop.

Later, I Googled the lyrics to "Wish You Were Here," which begin with the line, "So you think you can tell . . ."

So, here's what I think I can tell: We're all souls, sometimes missing a beat, and needing all of today's grace, hoping to be here—really here—using our own voice tomorrow.

Conquistadors

Leaving our two-year-old son, Joey, with his aunt Barbara, John and I were about to conquer new territory when we took our first vacation away after becoming parents. Along on the trip to Cancun was my sister Ruth and her husband, Alex. After a few days of the comfort and familiarity of resort living, we decided to take a day trip to Chichén Itzá. We'd heard the ruins were phenomenal, and worth the drive.

In 1988, there was no highway from Cancun to Chichén Itzá, so we had to take rugged back roads for more than four hours one way. And since there were no iPhones, no Google or Yelp back in that day, we missed checking ahead for hours of operation.

When we finally arrived, the site was closed. The man at the gate said they'd open again in a few hours, after they'd finished setting up for a light show on the pyramids.

He told us the first evening show was narrated in Spanish, and the English-speaking show was not until after that, which meant it would be several hours later and then it would be dark—too late to see the ruins, which sure would ruin everything.

"Por favor, mi amigo." John pleaded with the guy to let us in since we'd driven so far—even offering him a bribe. I know, shocking.

With a face of defeat, John walked back to the car. The four of us were discussing our options when a short, observant local tapped on the window. He mentioned the bribe the first man declined. This guy was a little more open-minded. We'll call him Arturo.

Offering to hop in our car with us, he could show us a secret entrance into the ruins. We all looked at each other for visual agreement. It sounded like a good idea to us, and so we handed him the pesos.

Parking the car along the side of the road, we followed our confident lil' freelance guide through the thick forest toward a breach in the fence that led us to the Sacred Well. We recognized it from the movie *Against All Odds*, which we all had just coincidentally seen. (Spoiler alert: this was the same well Jeff Bridges tosses Alex Karras into.)

As we tipped our heads down for a fuller view, four uniformed *federales* with machine guns walked up behind us—tapping us on our shoulders, so to speak. A touch too excited, Arturo told us to hold up our cameras and to just keep saying "*Touristas.*" This worked, but we had to leave. We were like, *Oh yeah, that's fine; we've seen enough of this wishing well. Have a nice day. Wish you well.* (That it's more of a sacrificial well than a wishing well is really beside the point. It would have made no sense to say, "Sacrifice you well." That would have definitely stirred the pot.)

Later, back through the front gate like fine, upstanding tourists, we sat and watched the Spanish-narrated light show, until John and I decided to deviate once again and skulk around the backside of the pyramid.

Once you get a taste of the city, the suburbs don't quite cut it.

Later that night, it was just the four of us north-of-the-border rebels, cruising along on back roads headed to Cancun. Having not taken no from the gatekeeper, we relished our new street cred as we spotted small cans spaced out on each side of the road ahead of us, with fires burning inside. *Now that's strange,* we thought. Not slowing down (which would have been the logical thing to do), we learned the purpose of the cans as we hit the thick, barrel-like rope stretched across the road. With a THUD THUMP CRASH, we nearly took out the bottom of our rental. These were Mexico's answer to speed bumps.

Slowing down for the firelight, we skulked the rest of the way down the Yucatan peninsula—and to our Mayan suburbia, but with a story to tell about an ancient city and a wishing well. Had it not been for bribe-accepting Arturo the Opportunist, we'd have missed the opportunity for adventure. Our path lit, we were now going "home" a little bit changed—once touristas, now conquistadors.

Forgotten Identity

I'm sitting in the Modesto Municipal Airport in northern California, and up until about fifteen minutes ago, it was a ghost town. Now, there are seven others waiting for the flight to San Francisco—the only flight leaving anytime soon and, I think, the only destination from here all day. Slightly stunned, I took a video of the literally empty lobby when I arrived. Since 911, surveilling with a camera is pretty frowned upon, but here, there was not one TSA to wag their finger and bark at me.

The ticket agent said the Modesto airport is closing soon. Not enough traffic. You snooze, you lose, I guess.

Ready to board the plane, I'm reflecting on this past week—a week where I spent the majority of my childhood.

At a spontaneous mini-reunion with some of my high school (and in some cases, kindergarten) friends, we met for dinner at Firenze, an Italian restaurant in Oakdale. There were eight of us.

My friend JoAnne asked me if I still draw.

"Not so much. Hardly at all, really."

"Why not?"

"Distracted, mostly. Drawing took a back seat to the roles of adulthood."

JoAnne seemed genuinely disappointed, and her reaction warmed my heart. She generously complimented the artwork of my childhood, recalling my talent and how I was "the artist" in school. I silently reflected that I *was* kind of the go-to when something needed to be drawn, elementary years through graduation. I loved to draw. I liked the identity. "Artist" was my label, and I liked it. But now I deflected her compliments, downgrading her appraisal: "Yeah, I mostly just copied stuff."

Now I don't even copy stuff.

I realized as I spoke these words that JoAnne still thought of me as who I was. Was I still the girl she remembered? Who is more accurate, her or me?

I told her that I really need to pick up the pencil again, that I'd been threatening to do so for the past few years, now that my kids are out of the house, now that I have time. I just need to make the time. Truth is, I'm a little afraid, fearful I've lost some of the gift—that old, "You snooze, you lose" thing. I think there is some truth to it—that if you let your gift wither, it can die like a flower.

Or an airport.

Suddenly, here in the airport, I do want to pick up the pencil again, thanks to JoAnne's encouragement.

She probably hasn't given this conversation one more thought since our dinner. But here I am, sitting in a sparsely populated airport, thinking of the possibilities.

In Their Mothers' Eyes

May 13, 2007

There is an image emblazoned in my mind of my baby daughter's wide blue eyes looking up at mine as I cradled and nursed her. These were the eyes of love. Incomparable, unadulterated love.

Sometimes she paused and smiled, and milk leaked out the corner of her full mouth and dripped down the side of her little face. With her tiny hand wrapped around my finger, I was her world.

That was Then.

This is Now.

Although I try to stay in the moment these days, I wake up and am reminded that Mother's Day is just two days away and my mind wanders to what might be. John told me yesterday there is a surprise in store, and that I need to get dressed up for Sunday. I wonder what I'll wear and if I need to buy pantyhose today. I only wear pantyhose for weddings and funerals, and now for a Mother's Day. I hate pantyhose.

I get my coffee, quickly check my email, and look at my calendar. My bed is unmade, and I flip on *The Today Show* while I gather up my sheets.

I see the crowd at Rockefeller Plaza standing at the edge of the barricade. Trying to get Al Roker or Matt Lauer's attention, they mug for the camera. I do this too, one long weekend every fall for the past few years. I tend to make a fool of myself, but I don't care. Some might see it as beneath their dignity. For me, it's an exercise in *carpe diem*.

It's a Mother's Day-themed show today, and the crowd is a sea of estrogen, with mother - daughter teams celebrating the holiday. I remember a couple New York trips ago, when Cassie and I were there. We were the semi-fearless California girls, taking the subway all over New York in every direction: up to Harlem for Sylvia's Soul Food, to Coney Island and beyond. We walked along the boardwalk and ate funnel cake, comparing the Atlantic beach to our Pacific.

Fridays are typically concert days on the plaza, and Meredith Viera introduces the recording artist, Martina McBride. The she-crowd cheers. While I am not what you'd call a country music fan, I stop collecting the sheets that have fallen to the floor and sit on the edge of the bed. The title, "In My Daughter's Eyes," catches my attention.

As Martina sings, the camera pans across the audience, capturing moments.

There is the young mother with her toddler. The little girl's head fits in the crook of her mommy's neck, and it is as if they are alone in her nursery, no shrill crowd around. In her tiny hand she holds an inflatable NYC souvenir, and as she snuggles her mommy, she lazily sucks on the end. Every time the camera revisits the duo, the intimate snuggle remains the same. Both mother and child are content—serene—as though there is nothing better anywhere else on the planet.

I wonder if there is. I don't think so.

In contrast, I notice something else—a dynamic that repeats itself within the crowd: One forty-something mom is proudly smiling at her daughter, tenderly rubbing her shoulder. The daughter looks elsewhere, captivated by the energy of the city, oblivious to her mother's touch.

There is another pair standing side by side: A daughter who stands several inches taller than her mother—she too is looking off in another direction. The mother, noticing that the camera is on them, cranes her neck upward to plant a kiss on her daughter's cheek. She is unable to reach her, and her daughter remains unaware of her mother's attempt at connection as the camera moves on.

Operative words: *moves on*.

The camera continues to survey the crowd as they listen to the lyrics. A look of adoration and reflection on the mothers' faces reveals a special moment to savor, for young and old alike. I notice something else, however, with the older moms who stand next to their coming-of-age daughters: a look of loss. Their eyes convey an impending goodbye—of reluctant acceptance that their daughter's gaze is elsewhere. Their daughters are growing up. The term *fear of abandonment* comes to mind.

I have had that look. I imagine so, anyway. I know I've had a lump in my throat at moments when I am dealing with my separation anxiety—when I realize the tiny hand that once held mine so tightly is trying to break free. While I know this is natural and normal and part of "the plan"—which is what I want—it hurts worse than I could have ever imagined. This process of letting go seems anything but natural. Much like childbirth itself.

I think back on myself when I left my mother's home. I too was oblivious. But it was nothing personal about my mom.

Making my bed, I notice the stack of Cassie's high school graduation announcements that need to be addressed and sent out. My baby daughter graduates high school in a few weeks. After that, there will be a busy summer. So far, I have not allowed myself to think beyond that, about her leaving for college, moving away, moving on.

I probably need to.

I will need to think this through; imagine the scenario. I should really visualize the packing; anticipate hearing the excited plans as the day looms closer. The day when my little girl lets go of my finger, and she looks away.

Therein Lies the Rub

John and I were at the Chinese twenty-dollar "foot massage."
I don't know why it's called the foot massage, because they spend equal amounts of time on the rest of the body. Unlike the massages at one of your more lavish spas, here you're fully clothed, in a group room; people are walking in and out, coughing; you can hear the phone ringing on the other side of the curtain, Mike-the-desk-guy-who-also-gives-massages explaining driving directions and prices, others chatting in the waiting area, customers whispering in some fashion. Also, the person next to you might be snoring. So there are drawbacks. But it's totally worth the twenty bucks.

The place is compartmentalized by curtains. There is the main room in the center, and then there are smaller rooms (with curtains) along the perimeter. I've never done it, but you can upgrade—pay more and have a "private" room. The only room I'm aware of that has an actual door is the bathroom. Yay for that, but you can still hear a person pee. There's something so vulnerable, so "It takes a village" about that.

This time, apparently, it was a slow massage day, and John and I were on our respective tables with the place to ourselves. I jumped to conclusions and thought, *This is gonna be nice.* But then there was a customer (pre-massage, from what I could tell) in a curtained, private room five-ish feet away, who decided he needed to place a phone call RIGHT NOW and contest a bill of some sort.

It's hard to gauge time when you are getting angrier by the second, but it seemed like he carried on that conversation for a minimum of fifteen minutes while he waited for his service. Or given his lack of manners, maybe the massage therapist was waiting for him.

I did the thing where I sat up and looked in the direction of the booming rude dude, being all exasperated, shaking my head, making eye contact with the therapist. This inspired a *Shhhhhhh* from her. Not even a *SHHHhhhhhhhh!!* Just a *Shhhhhhh*. No exclamation, only a meager period. At least it was something.

After another couple of minutes listening to his rant, I said, loudly, to John, "Is that a customer? I think it's a customer, right?" He shook his head and smiled an *I-don't know-but-I-hear-ya, this-stinks* smile.

Still more diatribe from Rude Dude. This time I addressed the massage therapist: "Do you speak English?"

She smiled sweetly and offered, "Tiny."

"Okay, is that a customer?"

She did a nod-shake. What does a nod-shake even mean? It's circular.

I laid my head back down, with one laser-eye burning into to the curtain, waiting for the man to appear so that I could verbally pounce. I knew exactly what I would say. I practiced it in my head: "DO YOU THINK YOU ARE ALONE IN HERE?!" I mean, that would get him.

And I totally would have said that, but he didn't exit while we were there. *Coward.*

My massage therapist motioned to me that it was time to turn over, and my mind went to *Turn the other cheek, Pam.* (*Cheek*, get it?) As in, *Get over it. You're adding to the ruin of this twenty-dollar massage. Yeah, he's inconsiderate, and self-centered. But turn the other cheek. That is all.*

I responded to my inner dialogue, *Yeah, but . . .*

No buts.

You don't understand, I argued. *It's not fair. He needs to know how he affects others. He needs to learn. I paid my twenty bucks. Who does he think he is?*

I thought of the scene in *Bridesmaids* when Kristen Wiig's character pulls the curtain separating first class from coach and indignantly says, "It's civil rights." I wanted to do that.

When our time was up, John and I put our sandals on, paid our fee plus tip, smiled sweetly at Mike-the-desk-guy-who-also-does-massage, and walked out. "See you next time," I said.

My anger dissipated, it was replaced by a peacefulness that I hadn't spoken up, hadn't said something I'd regret.

I had just wanted a twenty-dollar massage and a teensy bit of quiet. But we're simply not alone on this planet, even if we're separated by a curtain and oblivious to our impact.

And therein lies the rub.

Pulp Friction

Cold sweat, hands on hips, I stared him down. I waited. A minute. Two minutes. Five. And then I broke the silence. Someone had to. I said, "Oh, you wanna go?"

It's *mano a mano*.

Let's just say I had a slight run-in with the juicer yesterday morning. One of us has bruises.

I'm not kidding.

If your goal is conflict resolution, all good relationship experts say, "Begin with 'I' statements"—though not the way I've interpreted "I" statements in the past (i.e., "I feel like you're a jerk," "I hate you," etc.). A good therapist will also recommend an apology should not begin with "I'm really sorry you're such an idiot." Even when it's between you and a juicer.

Some background: I started this relationship with an uncomfortable but essential honesty. I said to my new juicer, "Buddy, I just wanna be healthy, ya know? No more of this leftover gnocchi before breakfast, quick-fried in a pan, crispy outside, tender in, topped off with a nice imported parm and a liberal douse of red picante flakes. I'm in menopause. Metabolism? They should call it *metabopause*. I need you. I need to get *green*. And not just green, *organic*. If the stuff ain't organic, it ain't goin' in ya. I don't care if it's spinach or bok choy. I have standards. For you, just the good stuff." (Side note: spinach is ridiculous to juice.) And for a long time, we were good.

Then I got impatient. Lazy. *You* try and juice four bunches of dandelion greens without a little celery tomfoolery. Sure, I cut corners. I admit it. The standard-issue apparatus plunger didn't cut it. Using a celery stalk to force the dandelion greens became more than a habit. Some might call it dependence; some, abuse.

My juicer's manufacturer had someone like me in mind, I'm guessing—a contingency plan for the impatient. If my juicer is jammed, there is a convenient "reverse" setting. Without getting too technical, typically all I need to do is press that bad-boy button and the greens regurgitate. And then, I force them down again with my ingenious celery plunger. Round two, or whatever.

So, yesterday we battled like never before—and sure—I got my juice. Pulpy, vomitus, organic, green, slimy, regurgitated sludge. I've become a sludge hammer.

That jammed juicer.

Battles and all, I still say: Take the plunge. Use the right tools. Juice for good health.

Go easy. Never force it. Be nice.

Smooth, sweet juice only comes with love.

Garage Key

In a neighborhood outside Detroit, a man broke into another man's garage. Pete Capone, the homeowner, caught the young man while he was inside, attempting to steal some carpentry tools. These were tools Pete used to make a living.

He told the robber that he was welcome to them, but he didn't need to steal them. Pete reached into his pocket, pulled out his keyring, took off the garage key, and extended it to him.

He extended the key.

The young man accepted the key, though he did nothing to deserve it. Some might say he deserved some punishment.

Later, a family member saw the guy return. He appeared to be testing the key to see if it worked.

It did.

He didn't open the door; he just left quietly.

That man showed up at Pete's funeral years later, telling family members that from that day on, he wore the key around his neck as a reminder of Pete's kindness, and he never stole again. He went into the carpentry trade. He said that unexpected grace changed his life.

My husband's Uncle Pete lived across country, so I only had the pleasure of meeting him a few times—but it didn't take more than a moment to know what an extraordinary man he was. Like another man, his side job was a carpenter; his main job was love. That's how he made a living.

Uncle Pete practiced grace as he moved a short time on this earth, emitting a light, a humble yet confident, unusual gentleness.

He extended mercy and trust, and offered brotherhood. And that's the key.

Fratello e Sorella

"I'm not doing too good as far as good is concerned."
—My Uncle Frank's response to my mom asking how he's been

I had just dialed my mom's number for Uncle Frank so they could catch up, brother-sister/ *fratello-sorella* style. I sat next to him on the dual La-Z-Boy couch that he had brought with him when he recently moved into his daughter Amaya's home after the passing of his wife of sixty-nine years. I sat in Aunt Edith's place.

I could hear his side of the conversation and much of my mom's side, since her voice carries, Italian-style. He continued, "I lost my best friend, Jean," as if he were telling her for the first time. His voice cracked.

I could hear my mom's familiar, compassionate tone. "I know, Frank."

For about fifteen minutes he spoke of the loss of Aunt Edith, asked about my dad, and he and my mom traded war stories about how hard it is to get older, how their bodies are failing, betraying them. Sentences that started like, "When my teeth fell out . . ."

A few times when his voice gained strength, I heard a familiar passionate quality and recalled the cadence of Uncle Frank's preaching voice. Growing up, I had heard it many times from the pulpit.

The conversation was drawing to a close, and Uncle Frank said, "We love you too. All right, be careful. Bye-bye."

He handed me the phone, and we sat a little longer and chatted. In this space, my heart expanded and broke.

One of his sweetest pet phrases is "Oh, golly gee . . ." and then he trails off. Bearing the weight of his head in his hand, he repeated, "Oh, golly gee . . . I don't know. I don't know what I'm going to do." This was in reference to living on without his beloved Edith. At one point when he said it, he started to cry.

And so did I.

A few moments later, he shifted and asked about my kids, how John's doing—he smiled as he asked, genuinely wanting to know.

The smile rose on his handsome face. I told him what a good-looking man he is, and how I'd remembered seeing photos of when he was young and how much he looked liked Clark Gable. I said, "I bet you sure had a lot of young women flirting with you."

The corners of his mouth turned up. "Oh, I don't know about that. I don't think so. I talked to some girls in Detroit and Pennsylvania. They didn't like me. But Edith, she did. She was a good one." And then the corners turned down again.

I told Uncle Frank about how much my mom admires him and what a wonderful brother he has been to her.

I love the way my mom beams when she speaks of her family and what it was like to grow up in their home. She could be talking about anything, and then I ask about her home, her parents, her brothers and sisters: her face lights up as if I'd flipped a switch. I don't think I've heard anyone talk about their brothers with such admiration, reverence, and respect. So often I've heard her say, "My *brother* Frank . . ." landing on "brother" with such a sense of pride, as if the word itself is a pure term of endearment.

My mom and Uncle Frank are the remaining two of seven siblings, and they chatted as soul survivors, *amici d'infanzia, fratello e sorella*, memory holders, seers of the long view, perhaps with a half-squinted eye on sharing a home together once again—reunited with their family who have gone on before, those who are achingly missed—while still holding the arm of a La-Z-Boy here.

Up in Smoke

Had the two Yosemidiots gotten wind of the forest fire, the one that ranked among the top three largest wildfires in California history? Sure they had. It had been on the national news. But reservations had been made, and so they had no reservations.

Once they opened the doors of their Mini Cooper—a Cooper bearing the weight of a kayak longer than the Cooper itself—they gasped. It's true what they say: "Where there's fire, there's smoke." The pair squinted as they looked up to the hazy grandeur of not just El Capitan, Half Dome, and Sentinel Rock but Yosemite Falls, Nevada Falls, and Vernal Falls. They noticed, however, that the water"falls" seemed to be *not* falling, which of course made them Failing Falls.

This should have been clue number one that the water in the Merced River—which runs through the valley and which these falls feed into—would be sparse at best. But these adventurers had come to Yosemite to kayak and to hike, come fiery hell or low water. For they call themselves "push past" types, a phrase coined by the wife. We'll call her, affectionately, Yosemite Pam.

The husband, "The More Reasonable One," who was not so psyched about the hike, suggested there is no way—*no way!*—they can hike today, and that it would be *yosemnutty*. However, he declared, "We can kayak today, maybe hike tomorrow."

Yosemite Pam acquiesced, for she is nothing if not submissive. Silent in her self-pity, she soldiered on, stiff upper lip, and put a smile on her ashy face.

Having made the earlier decision to hotel camp on this trip, they drove a bit longer down the road to the lodge, checked in, unpacked, and headed back to the launching point for the kayak adventure, sans water socks. Yosemite Pam distinctly remembered asking The More Reasonable One to pack her water socks.

It should be noted that the kayak, with its convenient hatches, stores items such as drinking water, snacks, first aid, iPhones, etc. The more water-sensitive items are housed within a rather expensive waterproof bag that can be snugly tucked into the hatches. This is double insurance, as the hatches themselves are airtight. But The Reasonable One and Yosemite Pam played it safe.

Yosemite Pam loves photography, especially in nature—God showing off. So you might see the dilemma with which she was faced: How could she take photos while the camera is relegated to a thick yellow bag? She'd spot a mama deer and her two fawns on the sandy shore, or notice the way the sunlight glistened on the shallow water and all those prominent rocks and logs. You have to be an awfully quick draw to get that iPhone out fast enough to catch these jewels in God's crown. Suffice it to say, the camera phone did not stay put in the thick yellow bag.

Their arrival down the river was entertaining for onlookers. All of them, of course, were on the river's edge; none were actually *on* the water. Some were shaking their heads. Perhaps they knew it was too late in the season for kayaking on a dry river.

Also clear to the bystanders was the chivalry of The More Reasonable One (hereafter known as TMRO; Yosemite Pam is now YP). They both did their fair share of paddling, but most of the time, TMRO had no choice but to disembark the watercraft and drag YP's sorry sass. When the bottom of the kayak could be heard loudly scraping and screeching along the river bottom, YP also abandoned ship, to the chagrin of the chivalrous.

"Just stay in. I'll pull you," he would plead, but she would have none of that.

There were times when the tattered, empty canoe completely

stalled, refusing to be dragged, and TMRO literally had to pick up the kayak and place it on his handsome and smart and sensible head. This was the only way to carry it over logjams, massive rocks, sand bars, and pizza restaurants.

This was no *The River Wild* movie, no Meryl Streep and Kevin Bacon here. This was like watching a dwarf sea horse documentary—the world's slowest fish, a fish that swims one foot every five minutes.

Hours later, and both of them finally back in the kayak, TMRO and YP saw the end in sight and breathed a sigh of relief. "Yes! We've made it!" they congratulated each other. As the twosome paddled toward the finish, they spotted a tricky passage ahead—and shrugged it off. After what they'd just endured, surely they would handle this as well.

Drawing closer, they could see the labyrinth: a submerged base of a tree next to an angling, sprawling, head-high branch from the river's edge. The sunken tree had moss-covered roots sticking up just above the water line. It looked like something out of an Edgar Allen Poe poem or a Tim Burton movie.

The fearless and unflagging captain TMRO, steering from behind and toward the side of the tree, which was in deeper water, attempted to navigate the obstacle course. Their best guess of what happened next was that there was a deceptive root at just the right wrong angle. That, combined with the sudden pressure of the current in the deeper water—water deeper than any they had yet encountered all day—became the perfect storm, if you will.

You know the side of the kayak with seats? That side of the kayak was upside down. And the side that had been scraping against rocks and pebbles and trees for hours? Well, that was right-side-up.

It was a slow-motion flippage of "this is not happening" proportions, only yards from their destination, where they would have arrived dry but for their wet and torn feet. Sure, TMRO's back was racked with pain, and his head was bruised from the weight of the kayak. Still, they would've fist pumped for having beaten the river.

Oar not.

As they both came up for air, it was not clear if TMRO's first words were, "Are you alright?" or "Where's your iPhone?" YP knew exactly where it was, for it was near and dear to her—in her pocket, also known as the watery grave, close to her sopping soul.

Looking at the once-vibrant iPhone with the Capone family photo screensaver, all she saw was black. Using John's iPhone to Google how to resurrect a drowned iPhone, they learned that rice might do the trick, and so as soon as was humanly possible, they rushed to the Yosemite General Store. The phone, now comatose, was packed in white rice and, ironically enough, placed in that thick yellow waterproof bag. A vigil was held, not so much for the phone itself, but for the photos of God's good stuff.

Day two meant hiking to Glacier Point, also known as "The Four Mile Trail," which TMRO pointed out is a misnomer, since it's actually 4.6 miles and a 3,200-foot ascent from the valley floor. He also warned how unhealthy it would be to hike while breathing smoke of such wildfire magnitude, referring to it as "smoke inHellation." He spoke of the possibility of respirators, bronchitis, asthma, emphysema, impaired lungs, iron-lung machines, rescue teams that could cost five thousand dollars. YP had a vague sense TMRO's heart was not in it.

Now at the trailhead, as YP bent down to lace up her boots, her trusty and beloved Maui Jim sunglasses fell from her head—literally a few inches—hitting soft dirt and splitting in two at the bridge. This adventure had proven and over and over again to be a comedy of errors.

The climb was not exactly a breeze. Both TMRO and YP had hiked to the top of Half Dome the summer before, but here they were suckin' air. Smoky air. YP kept her unflagging sense of humor, noting how funny it is when hikers pass one another and say "High." Of course it's high—that's why it's called a mountain. *Duh.*

After a little over three hours, they made it to the top. This particular hike leads to a lookout point (Glacier Point) that typically has views of the famous mountain ranges, but it is also accessible by vehicle. Which means accessible by bus, which means there might be a shuttle bus that could—potentially—take hikers back down into the valley via mountain road.

TMRO's and YP's eyes lit up as they discussed the idea of returning on this shuttle. Then they realized they had missed the last one of the day by twenty minutes. Twenty. Minutes. They were crestfallen.

YP suggested for the first time in her life that she would venture into the risky world of hitchhiking. "See that parking lot over there?" she pointed. "Maybe we should scope out some old people who are much less likely to be mass murderers and ask them if they are headed back into the valley. We can offer them money. Friendship. Undying gratitude."

TMRO and YP did catch a ride, but not with senior citizens; it was with non-slasher, non-hockey-mask-wearing Minnesotans. After an hour car ride down a zigzagging road, their new friends would only accept their friendship. They were a match made in Yosemite.

That night TMRO and YP drove to their next destination, Wawona, an historic hotel built in the late 1800s. YP took a bath in a clawfoot tub, one of her favorite things on this fabulous planet. She even took a photo of it with TMRO's iPhone, which she kept a good distance from the water. The next day they limped, hobbled, nursed their wounds, lounged on Adirondack chairs, spoke with the friendly locals and visitors alike. YP mentioned she thought park rangers were some of the nicest people around. "It must be their nature," she said.

TMRO and YP went for a swim in the retro rectangular pool and sunned themselves a bit. Beeware, though, if you visit the Wawona. As YP climbed out of the pool and onto the grass, she stepped on a bee and was stung. The More Reasonable One, the chivalrous love of Yosemite Pam's life, ran to her aid, fetched ice and baking soda, and looked for that bee they both secretly hoped was dying a torturous death. That tricky, horrible bee. Sure, she loves honey, who doesn't? For that, they're grateful, but honey, enough is enough, and they were plum out of puns.

The Nerve

Before opening my eyes that October morning, I knew I could not lift my head off the pillow without excruciating pain. I vaguely remembered waking in the middle of the night and feeling a stiff neck, but had fallen back asleep. I had no idea this was brewing. John was away on business.

Alone and literally screaming, it took me a half an hour to slide my body down off the bed and get to the bathroom. I had given birth to two babies, each time with back labor that an epidural couldn't touch, and endured an ankle surgery and months of therapy that made me see stars, but the hurt that was shooting from my neck down into my body was the most horrendous physical pain I had ever experienced. I laid in bed, essentially paralyzed, until John came home the next day, when he took me to the emergency room.

After two heavy-duty Dilaudid shots and an MRI, the doctor ruled out anything wrong with my spine, and sent me home with muscle relaxers and painkillers and the most relieving news that this would be temporary. Maybe three or four days. He diagnosed it as a severe muscle spasm in my neck that had pinched a nerve—a nerve that sent me into the depths of what I like to call a short visit to hell.

While I lay in bed recovering, I had time to count my blessings and put things in perspective. After returning from his business trip, John played nurse to me while he battled his own horrible bout with the flu. As he helped me lift my head out of bed, I could smell his fevered, stinky, sick breath, and it made me love him all the more.

Over the next few days, with the aid of drugs and time, I began to get my mobility back, even though for the most part I could only turn my head to the right, which meant it took some effort to avoid going in circles. My sense of humor was returning also.

Heading out to get a prescription filled for me, John spotted Riley and Bradley and another boy playing in the street in front of our house. Brothers Riley and Bradley, now eight and nine years old, were basically our adopted boys. They'd been part of our family since they were two and three. They'd come over, ask what's for dinner, swim in our pool, watch Jim Carey's *The Grinch* with me in the middle of summer, leave the toilet lid up, and eat chips with me in the hammock. They were our boys. So as John backed out of the garage, Riley motioned to him to roll down the window.

"Hey, John, I just rang the bell and no one answered."

"Yeah, Pam couldn't get to the door. She's had a really bad pain in her neck and has had a hard time moving. Maybe you guys could say a prayer for her."

Bradley and the other boy, who were in earshot, sort of nodded and went back to playing, but John could see in Riley's eyes that this penetrated him.

"I'll pray!" Riley said, and without saying goodbye, he darted across the street to the middle of a neighbor's lawn, a lawn that's something of a grassy knoll—nothing hidden or obscured. He knelt down dead center at the lawn's highest point, folded his hands in front of his face, bowed his head, and began to pray. He didn't at all seem to care who saw him.

As John drove down the street, he kept watch in his rearview mirror. Riley continued to pray the stretch of the entire block.

The nerve, the pure faith of a child: he wanted God to heal me, and he knew where to go.

Nerve is a funny thing. It can debilitate you, and it can move you.

Night Train to Nice

Our family did things on the cheap, like camping. We had a lot of fun when the kids were small, but there was no extra money for big vacations. They did have Disneyland passes when they got a little older, but those were generally the big Christmas or birthday gift, or supplied by their grandma. These were not spoiled kids. And they never fought. I can say "never" with practically no caveat. I could probably count on half a finger how many times Joey and Cassie fought growing up.

Our first official family trip was to Maui in 2002, which was a big deal. A couple years later, when we said we were going to Europe, it was huge. While we had turned a corner financially, we still needed to be frugal. I wasn't thrilled that John bought each of the kids an iPod for the trip. I saw this as extravagant.

In any case, it wasn't tough to find rooms that would accommodate four people in Italy, but France was another story. We knew we'd end up having to rent two rooms there, in our final few days before heading home.

John's the consummate travel agent, our go-to if we need anything. We rely on the guy. A complete Type A, his forte is figuring things out ahead of time, nailing down the details—he does a PowerPoint, if that tells you anything—and his thought was for us to take the night train from Venice to Nice, which would accomplish two goals: transportation and lodging for one night.

Having just celebrated Joey's eighteenth birthday in Venice that day, we boarded our train to Nice. John had never traveled by train before, so when he bought four third-class sleeper-car tickets, he didn't think much about it—other than we'd be saving money on a hotel. Score!

When we found our teeny compartment, it had a pair of three-seat couchettes facing each other along the wall of the car, with about a foot and a half in the middle for a walkway. Above the entry door was a space for luggage, which would not even come close to the space we'd need for our bags. I warned John about not packing so many curling irons and shoes. Men!

The couchettes converted into beds. Those two berths, along with the two additional beds over each couchette that folded down, made for a bottom, middle, and top bunk, which meant this sleeper compartment was designed for six munchkins from Oz. John had only purchased four berths. I'm not much for division, but even I knew there was a remainder.

When the two strangers-who-were-about-to-sleep-with-us arrived, they took one look at our family wedged into that space, along with our collective luggage, and did an about face. They said they'd look to see if there were any vacant compartments. Good call. They never returned.

Joey and Cassie had chosen to fight—essentially for the first time in their lives—in Italy, the place I'd wanted to see, and taste, since forever. There, they bickered.

And bickered.

And bickered.

With about ten days' build-up, my frustration erupted in the middle of the piazza in the most beautiful place, my Happiest Place On Earth: San Gimignano, Tuscany. I came undone. Standing in front of a *salumi* and *formaggi* shop with its wild boar's head over the entry, I turned into a wild boar mama, complete with Italian hand gestures before a frigillion locals and tourists. I may have used the word *selfish* multiple times.

No one responded. There was just a lot of stare-down activity, including the wild boar's head. It was quite the ironic situation.

During our last day in Venice, things had smoothed out for Joey and Cassie. Settling in to our sleeper car, I noticed the kids playing Rock Paper Scissors. I admitted to them that I never understood the game, and they thought that was hilarious.

Someone thought it would be fun to document that admission with a camcorder, and then school me in the time-honored game. I redelivered my line, "What are you doing?" but I was unable to pull off a very good acting job because I kept laughing. I finally managed, "What are you guys playing?

"Rock Paper Scissors, Mom," says Cassie.

More uproarious laughter, and then I say, "I don't understand . . . I don't understand that game." Okay, so my strength is not in my acting.

Ever the encourager, Cassie says, "Mom, it's not hard."

"How do you play that game?" I ask. (For some reason, we all think this is riotous and cannot keep it together.)

Joey summons an authoritative tone: "Oh, Mother, it's the simplest game of all the land. It's used to settle small disputes . . ." There are ongoing eruptions of laughter, questions, and suggestions on how best to go forward with our reenactment.

Interrupting his sister, Joey continues, "When two persons come into a dispute, and they find themselves unable to reconcile, sometimes they either call for a flip of a coin, or a game of Rock Paper Scissors. It's an old game, an ancient game . . . invented by the Greeks, I believe . . ."

The video then cuts to John sitting on his top bunk, smiling, and then the camera unsteadily pans our sleeper compartment, where you see me fumbling to get my bag down. Joey asks his dad if he will say something into the camera, to which John replies, "Something." He smiles and continues, "This is a wonderful camping event. We're sweating; Mom's freezing; it's a beautiful thing."

Joey, the true actor in the family, turns the camera on himself and begins his soliloquy:

"Today's my eighteenth birthday, and I'm about to have the worst night's sleep I've ever had in my entire life. This has now become my photo diary . . . I'll periodically make updates as I see fit." There is a dramatic pause, and then, "I don't know what else to say."

Even though I knew John was overheated, I requested for about the forty-seventh time that the window be closed, and in the video you can see we hadn't even started moving yet. The vibe was that we were in for a long night.

Knowing my struggles with insomnia, I had packed Tylenol PM. The first and last time I ever pushed drugs on my children, I asked them if they'd like some help getting through the night. I didn't love that Joey was recording me, but he reassured me it's just going to be us seeing it. I did NOT feel like getting a call from Nice's social services.

There is a cut-away, and then back again to more jerky camera work, when Joey requests a recounting of what had just happened while the camera was off regarding John's aggressive handling of Cassie's bag.

Joey asks his dad, "Now tell me, why were you inclined to throw Cassie's bag on the ground?"

"She really frustrated me." He's frugal *and* forthcoming.

"So basically, the thought in your head was *Cassie's frustrating me; I'm going to break her iPod and her camera.*"

"Exactly."

"Dad, be honest with me, a little true confessional here. If that door was big enough and you had the trajectory—if you had the angle—right, would you throw her bag out the window?"

I chose not to comment on the incongruence of the window

and door hypothetical.

"Absolutely not," John says.

"Why?"

"'Cause I paid for that stuff." We're back to the money.

"But you threw it down. You wanted to break it."

"I didn't throw it down; I dropped it."

"You threw it. Cassie said you threw it. You threw it."

"Cassie's mistaken."

"But Dad, I saw it drop."

"I saw it drop too," John admits.

"I saw your hands. And then I saw your hands off of it and I saw it drop."

Sounding a tad snarky, John says, "And you even have it on tape."

"I don't have it on tape."

"You should."

Having had enough, John begins to remove his jeans and get underneath the sheets. Joey comments that things are getting scandalous.

You can hear me in the background saying, "Hey, John, how do you close this window? I'm freezing . . ." and then Cassie saying, "Dad, will you take a picture of me and NOT throw my camera on the ground?"

John groans an "Oh geez."

Like fine-oiled machinery, the three of us children make simultaneous, rapid-fire requests of John, with a nice touch from Joey: "Hey Dad, hey Dad, hey Dad, hey Dad, hey Dad, hey Dad, hey Dad, do something for me"—all building, of course, into a nicely executed crescendo and, perhaps, the piece de resistance from Cassie: "Dad, will you take a picture of my flowing hair?!"

Poor guy. Poor, longsuffering, detail-oriented, hot, frugal guy.

Right before the video fades to black, you can hear Joey say, "This will be the chapter entitled 'Dad's Nightmare.'"

I still don't really understand the Rock Paper Scissors game, but if it's an effective dispute settler, then I'm all for it.

It was the berth of a new era for us—just a simple, nice family trip to Nice.

Stolen Answers

"You want to give it ten more minutes?" John asked me in the dark.

"Alright," I said, one-fourth-heartedly, not even half. The plasma TV screen illuminated John's disinterested face.

We were about thirty minutes into a pay-per-view movie with Russian subtitles, a film that the review website Rotten Tomatoes had given a 99 percent. Ratings don't get much higher than that. It seemed like a sure thing, but so far we both were underwhelmed, trudging through the dialogue and subtitles and depressing visuals. It was getting more and more difficult to be motivated to read. I had actually begun scanning. That's not a good thing if you want to follow a plot.

Now I have to really dislike a movie to bail on it, but I couldn't make it ten more minutes and told John I was done trying. He agreed, and we shut it off, calling it a night. I didn't care that we were wasting our money; we were wasting minutes of our lives we'd never get back, and so we may as well cut our losses.

The next day I was on the elliptical looking for something to watch to distract from my workout, and landed on a thumbnail and description that looked interesting. Plus, I loved the cast. Normally I consult Rotten Tomatoes before investing time in a movie, but decided to give it a shot without doing my homework. I hadn't even thought about the night before and the fact that my trusted film review website had failed me. I just didn't want to take the time to go to my laptop.

I loved this movie. I loved it so much that after I completed my hour on the elliptical, I sat sweaty and watched it through to the closing credits. It was a film about the search for happiness, which was perfect because it made me happy.

Curious to see what Rotten Tomatoes had to say about this one, I was shocked to see the 36 percent rating. The critics said it was sentimental garbage. I normally eschew predictable, cloying cinema. But this didn't feel like that. Sure, it wasn't perfect, but it was—dare I say it—life affirming. It seemed honest.

It occurred to me that perhaps I have been relying too heavily on Rotten Tomatoes, strictly adhering to my "Never watch anything that's rated below 60 percent rule." Maybe I had been missing lots of good stuff because I had been accepting something someone told me, lazily trading what I might think for what someone else thinks—someone who had their own biases, someone who had made up their mind. I was routinely going with the majority consensus, and I didn't know it until I caught myself doing it.

I remember once in eighth-grade science class when a majority of us students were in on a scheme to cheat on a big test. It turned out the teacher had suspected ongoing cheating, so he planted a sheet on his desk that appeared to be the answers to an upcoming test, and then left the room for a bit. One student saw the answers and passed them on to the rest of the class, which we then "helped" one another glean during the examination, Domino-style. My friend strategically placed his paper near the edge of the desk so that I could clearly see it, and I copied it. Then I moved my paper to the edge for my neighbor.

The answers were all wrong.

Most of the class failed the test. In more ways than one.

I cannot recall my teacher's name, but I remember exactly what he looked like and the fact that he used to brag about having a steel plate in his head. I don't remember how he got it.

What stands out most about him in my memory, though, was his look of satisfaction when he told us what he'd done, and what

107

he knew we'd done. He gloated, absolutely beaming when he said we'd fallen for his trap. You'd think he'd have been more saddened by it, but he seemed happy. It was kind of creepy, actually. I'm not sure whose behavior was worse, his or ours.

Stolen answers are not always the right answers. Neither are borrowed answers. Using the brain God gave me, I've found it's best to do my own work, keeping my eyes on my own paper.

The Exhortation Flatulation

As the preacher was exhorting his congregation, I heard a small toot near me, and then a quiet "Oops, excuse me."

The woman two seats down the *pee-yew* had just bent over to pick up something that had fallen out of her purse. Apparently she had eaten something quite gassy before church.

I pretended it didn't happen. Knowing my propensity to laugh at inappropriate times, I had to shift gears in my head—fully aware that if I allowed myself to think about it at all, it would be over for me. Setting my jaw, I deliberately looked ahead to avoid my husband's eye, and tried desperately to focus on what the pastor had just said—something about self-control.

I needed a good talking-to. *Focus, Pam, you're a grown-up. Think Sermon on the Mount and kindness. NO, think about poverty, AIDS, racism in America, ISIS, back labor, funerals. No, wait—not funerals! You've laughed during far too many funerals.*

I noticed a slight commotion in my periphery, directly behind the flatulent woman. Against my better judgment, I looked back and saw that another woman had heard the toot as well. Chortling, her body shaking, and with her hand over her mouth, I knew it was over for me. I lost it.

For once, though, I wasn't alone! I wasn't the only middle-aged woman struggling with spiritual maturity.

Even the apostle Paul had trouble with this one. In my interpretation, it's one of the more squirrely, relatable scriptures in the Bible. To the Romans, he's like (and I'm paraphrasing), "Hey, I'm just gonna put it out there—there's no good in me as far as my nature goes. I want to do what's right—I really do—but I can't. I don't want to do what's wrong, but I end up doing it anyway. Sheesh! So if

I do what I don't want to do, I am not really the one doing wrong; it's that crummy, no-good nature in me that's to blame. Blame THAT."

I'm all that and a bag of gas too. I need help. On my own, I can be a rambling mess.

Read the essence of what Paul's saying, and the word *scapegoat* might come to mind. If it does, perfect! If you look at the origin of *scapegoat*, it's from the Old Testament, when a goat was symbolically laden with the sins of the Israelites and sent into the wilderness as a sacrifice.

In other words, we have a scapegoat at our disposal, and that's not a bad thing. In fact, it's the very best thing.

It might sound chicken, as if Paul just doesn't want to own his choices, but he's merely being real and delusion-free: without a greater power outside himself, he's fighting an unwinnable battle.

Try as we might, things sneak out. Toots happen, and we laugh when we're not supposed to. Knowing ourselves—and accepting the help of grace—is one of the most grown-up things we can do.

The Crossover

As John was rushing around, dressing for work, I heard his booming voice approaching—all business, likely on an early-morning conference call. Sitting at my desk, I anticipated a quick kiss goodbye. I turned my face to him . . . and I was horrified. Bluetooth in his ear, John's dress pants were violently too high. We're talking dangerous levels. Lethal.

"What are you doing?! Why are your pants so high?!"

Interrupting his call, he whispered, "What? What are you talking about?" He looked down at his waist, shook his head as though *I* was the unreasonable one, and adjusted, then kissed my cheek and walked out. I heard the garage door go up.

That night when he got home from work, I cleared my throat and said, "John, we have to talk. You've crossed over. We must go back."

"Huh?"

"This morning. Your pants. They were up to your armpits. You've crossed over from cool surfer dude to old man. Snap out of it!"

He begged to differ. He felt it was all in my perception. Pointing to his current, acceptable belt-level situation, he said, "They were just like this."

I shook my head, "No. Thou doth protest too much, methinks." (Perfect Shakespearean application.)

The next morning I was lying on the floor doing my stretches when he came in, no conference call this time. I looked up. He was literally wearing his pants a la Steve Urkel, virtually up and over his areolas. Smiling.

He thought this was cute.

I screamed, grabbed at my eyes, and started rubbing feverishly. "Nooooooooo, nooooooo! Get me the bleach! Pour the Clorox directly into my eyes! You have no idea what you have just done to our love life! Stop it!!" I groaned for a ridiculously long time to make sure he got the message.

He went downstairs and I could hear him laughing. I heard the garage door go up.

I have never been able to understand the thinking of men who wear their pants far too high, but okay, I can accept it in certain contexts if I must. Chris Christie, okay. Joaquin Phoenix in the film *Her*, okay; that was a stylistic choice. I saw Clint Eastwood greet Ellen DeGeneres on her show, and I have to say, I noticed the pants. I wanted to say, "No, Dirty Harry. No, please, no. Make my day; make that whole look go away."

I don't remember a line in our wedding vows about the pants. I remember "in sickness and in heath, for richer or for poorer"—those kinds of things. Reasonable commitments. No caveats about hiking up your trousers when you crest Fifty Hill. It feels a little sudden and below the belt. What's next? Sandals and black socks? Bushy ear hair?

Pants brought us together in the first place back in August of 1982. John is the brother of my friend Cheryl, so I had known him for a while—actually, I'd been crushing on him for a while. We were at a beach party and my legs were cold, so he offered me an extra pair of Levi 501s he had in his pickup truck. A few days later, sitting at another bonfire—this time at a church camp—he said he'd like to get those jeans back, like, right now. He walked me back to my cabin, which turned out to be a ruse. Apparently, he was ready to crush back. I handed the jeans to him, and he planted one right on my kisser.

Thirty-one years in, I still think he's a pretty cool surfer dude, with his salt-and-pepper getting saltier. Just watch the waistband on those board shorts, John.

There may be a change or two he's noticed about me, but he hasn't said. If he has noticed, he wouldn't say. It's not his way.

Meanwhile, the garage door goes up, the garage door goes down—and we're still crossing over to each other.

This is Where You Are

My friend Stacie was diagnosed with a deadly, inoperable brain tumor. With no warning on New Year's 2013, she was told she had eighteen months to live.

There's a photo on my desk—right at eye level—of Stacie and her husband, Darren. She's resting her head on a pillow as she lies on a doctor's office table. All you see of Darren is his outstretched arm and his hand on her head. On his forearm is a visible tattoo that reads in block letters: THIS IS WHERE YOU ARE.

The photo is on my desk for a few reasons. Primarily selfish—I've been a grump this week with my husband (he may claim it's been two; who's to say?). I realized I need a reminder that moments are not guaranteed, and lately I was guilty of discarding too many.

I printed the picture out last night and told him I was sorry for my unlovely crankiness—and that we ought to treat one another like we're terminal.

Because we are.

We just forget we are. It's only a matter of how and when.

Darren posted the photo on Facebook a few days ago while he and Stacie were at Cedars-Sinai getting her treatment, and I've been inspired, troubled, and touched by it ever since.

INSPIRED because of the tender way I see Darren caring for Stacie every time I'm at their place. Every. Single. Time. And the way she looks at him—on Monday, the concerned way she asked him if he'd eaten lunch.

TROUBLED because I hate that she's sick. I can't imagine how much Darren or his and Stacie's kids or Stacie's parents or siblings hate it. There can't be a word for it.

TOUCHED because, I mean, how can I not be? I look at his

hand on her head—her precious head turned toward him, eyes shut, resting, allowing his touch to cover her cancer, that nasty thing trying to kill his sweet, funny, beautiful wife. On his wrist, a watch keeping time, moments. The tattoo on his arm—I'd noticed Darren's tattoo before but never asked what it meant. I assumed it meant to stay in the moment. I bet he's doing a lot of that, cherishing Stacie. Or maybe it means, "It is what it is." Or I wonder if he wants to rub that tattoo off his arm in defiance, as in, "NO, this is NOT where I want us to be! I want us to be anywhere but Cedars!"

But this is where they are, together.

I want a tattoo of this picture—this photo of what love looks like, what it really looks like. Recognizing my forgetful nature, and that five minutes from now is a mystery, I will embrace this moment, because this is where I am.

Pinched

The Italians have a cheek-pinching custom. Some of my uncles and aunts pinched me so hard as a little girl that if I saw them coming, I would run the other way. But now my cousin Amaya and I had to pinch each other to see if this was real. Did we really have an apartment in the Piazza della Signoria, steps away from the famed Uffizi Gallery and the Ponte Vecchio Bridge? For a month? And after Florence, another month of traveling down the stylish boot? It was all too wonderful.

Nearing the second full week in Florence, it had rained nearly every day. It didn't matter; I was living out a dream and nothing could dampen my spirits.

Waking to a scratchy throat, I decide to take a day off from the piazzas and lay low. I will run a few errands and then come back to the apartment and just chill. Maybe today will be the day I start sketching, and possibly make dinner with some sweet and savory goodies from the market.

I make my to-do list:

1. Bancomat (ATM).
2. Sant'Ambrogio Market (fresh pasta, produce, etc.)
3. Tailor (to pick up the two new leather jackets that should be ready. It's been chilly.)
4. Buy my beloved tomato bread soup at Francescano's for my achy throat.

Wearing a new leather jacket under my raincoat, my wallet now replenished, I walk unfazed in the pelting rain through our piazza, past the Fountain of Neptune, up the cobblestone streets through

Piazza Santa Croce, and alongside the basilica to the Sant'Ambrogio. I am thrilled to see that the outdoor produce market is teeming with people. I was under the impression that it was only open on Tuesdays, so this is a great surprise. I decide to buy the outdoor produce after I get the pasta and sauce from inside the market.

Inside there is robust Italian banter, laughter, and spontaneous singing—such an iconic picture of Italian life. Standing at the fresh pasta and cheese counter, I am rendered speechless by the beauty behind the glass, but then *tre* words come: Uh. Maze. Ing. I think angels are singing.

I take a number. Hearing only Italian spoken around me—from the patrons, the clerks, everyone—I suddenly get nervous about the language barrier and try and ramp up the self-talk: *You can do this, Pamelina. Oh, yes, you can.*

The pasta man calls my number, *quattordici.*
I jump in and ask, *"Si, parla inglese?"*
"No."

I smile, accepting what is. I point to the massive ravioli like my grandma used to make.

"Okay, *vorrei cinque ravioli, per favore."*

Pasta-man smiles and says, "Perfecto," impressed with my effort.

The next few items and quantities are not so easily articulated, and the man next to me takes pity on me and offers assistance. In his thick Italian accent he says, "I speak a little English; maybe I can help." He helps me buy three more pastas and two sauces. I love him. *People are good.*

Completely grateful for humanity at large, I thank everyone around me—*mi famiglia*—and we all say *ciao.* Head held high, I walk toward the exit and out to the produce where the raindrops fall on the canopy. I grab a couple of plastic bags and start collecting vegetables, like I would at the swap meet at home. As I do, I sense I might be getting the stink-eye from a woman standing nearby, and so, of course, I smile at her and try to diffuse any brewing conflict. Dale Carnegie training in action.

She does not smile back. I read her right.

I smile one more peace-making smile. She looks at me as though I am *il diavolo* stealing her six bambinos and dipping them in hot extra virgin olive oil and picante.

I reach for the tomatoes, and she pins me between the arugula and endive. I cannot move.

I am literally pinched between produce.

It seems too bizarre to be true, but it is. In her thick Italian-accented staccato she barks, "There is a queue!"

"Oh, I'm sorry. I didn't see a line."

She mocks me: "You're sorry, you're sorry. You're not sorry!"

"Yes, I *am* sorry. I did not understand."

"You understand! GO AWAY!"

I am stunned.

"That's not very nice," I mutter. I'm three years old.

I can feel the rain puddles forming in the back of my eyes, welling up. I tell myself, *C'mon Pammy, she's just a mean lady. Let it roll off your back.*

The produce man says something to me in Italian, and from his body language, I see that he's ready for me to pay for my spinach, tomatoes, and green onion. I am extricated from the woman and I hand him *tre* euro.

As I leave, the tears come. After fighting them and failing, I decide to let them come full force. I stand there in the rain holding my wet produce and pasta. I wonder, *Is it hormones? Is it the scratchy throat? Am I overtired?*

I decide not to question and just accept. After all, I've experienced a microcosm of human behavior in a market.

Having been pinched by an Italian, I walk directly into the rain, and not the other way. I pass through a sea of umbrellas and get whacked in the side of the head with one. Whacked so hard I feel my scalp with my wet fingertips, checking for blood. I cry a bit longer and then head to errand number three: the tailor, to pick up my two new leather jackets to keep me warm and dry.

You Do the Math

"Go to the chalkboard," the teacher said.

With the wide eyes of my classmates on me, my seven-year-old skinny legs stood rickety at the board. An oversized, dark, dusty eraser in my left hand, a thin stick of pure white chalk in my right, I didn't know the answer to the arithmetic problem. What's more, I didn't even know how to begin to do it.

None of my classmates made fun of me. It was the adult who did.

I can't recall her exact wording. Mostly what I remember was the way the tone felt in my ears, falling down into my heart.

The message was clear: I was bad for not knowing, not understanding. I sat down.

In the days and months and years that followed, I allowed myself to be limited in specific ways because of that very day. I absorbed the shame; I believed the lie. I made real-life choices because of her imprint.

And sometimes I catch myself, still, believing her lie.

It was a powerful day. She was a powerful person.

My sad little story is not an uncommon one. It doesn't add up why someone entrusted to teach and nurture would write such awful things on the chalkboard of young hearts.

I'm thankful for good teachers who love what they do; for big erasers, new sticks of chalk, and for brilliant quotes like this:

> *"Well, another day has passed and I didn't use algebra once."*
> UNKNOWN

And here's what I write on the chalkboard of my little heart these days:

> *"Don't let anyone else be that second-grade teacher."*

The Bag

What I think I know and what I truly know can be wildly different. I can laugh now at what I thought I knew at twenty-five. What I think I know more than twenty-five years later is probably just as laughable.

The long driveway leading to the IMA School is a vertical beast. At the top of the hill sits the campus, and to the back side of the walled campus is a dirt road that leads down into a dusty village where many country Guatemalans—and most of our IMA girls—live. Many people have to walk up the IMA driveway, passing the school, and then walk down into the village on the other side to get home.

Before the school day begins, I try and incorporate a workout. So far my routine this week includes a morning trek up and down The Beast ten times. This morning, on what was maybe my fifth ascent, I caught up with a native woman struggling to carry two sacks—a smaller one in her left hand and the larger one in her right, the hand nearest to me.

I saw that she was having to pause and rest, so as I got nearer to her, I reached out to take the bag nearest to me. She looked at me with raised eyebrows and "telepathed," *Are you sure you know what you're doing?*

She didn't want me to help, but I insisted. I played the American hero.

Smiling sweetly, she offered me the smaller bag instead. I work out regularly; surely this bag would be a piece of sweet corn cake. So I reached for the heavier one and uttered a cocky "*De nada.*" ("It's nothing.")

That sucker must've weighed forty pounds.

I was too proud or stubborn (or both) to give it back, and so of course I struggled up the hill with the bag. She could see my effort and tried to take it back. I agreed via Spanglish that it's *muy difícil* but it's okay; I want to help.

We finally got to the top and she thanked me, taking the bag again and heading down the backside of the hill into the village.

My puny American brain knows nothing of what it is to live in a developing country. I have visited many places and sometimes like to persuade myself that I've seen what it's like. I've seen it, sort of, but I haven't carried the weight. Which makes me think that at seventy-five I'll probably recognize the naivete of what I *thought* I knew today.

Can I Get a Witness?

Before heading over to my friend Stacie's house, I spoke with her husband, Darren, via cell to get specific instructions on what to pick up for Stacie since she is on a very specific diet to help fight her brain tumor. They would be heading home from a doctor's visit, and Stacie would be hungry, and Darren wouldn't have time to cook before he went to some work appointments. I would meet them at home with dinner, and then hang out with Stacie while Darren was gone.

I took notes:

Chicken bacon burger with guacamole.
Wrapped in lettuce.
No bun, aka " wrap."

Easy peasy. Darren said all the fast-food places are familiar with doing a wrap versus the bun, and specifically named Carl's Jr. Being a carb freak, this is new territory for *moi*. Hence the notes.

I walk into Carl's Jr feeling the chances are greater that the order will be done correctly eyeball to eyeball versus a drive-through with that whole speaker dynamic, static, and whatnot. Standing at the counter simultaneously looking at the vibrantly lit overhead menu and looking respectfully into the eyes of the teenage girl who will be taking my order, I say, "I would like a chicken burger. Do you have chicken BURGERS?"

With perhaps the most zombie-like response I have ever seen, she raises her arm says, monotone, "Here's what we have."

"I see that, but I can't tell by the picture if they are actual patties or breasts. Can you tell me if it is a patty like a burger, or is it an actual chicken breast?"

With her lethargy level deepening and digging in her heels, she raises and points once again, like a drugged Vanna White, and remarks, "Here are our chicken sandwiches."

We did this no less than four more times. I'm not kidding.

I'm a great tipper; I am super-polite to the service industry, because I've been there. But I was beginning to feel an internal transition. "I see the photos of all the chicken-type sandwiches; I need to know if it's like a burger or breast. I am bringing it to a sick friend and she is on a very strict diet. It's important for me to know what form this chicken will take."

Same catatonic answer.

I look around, thinking there's got to be a hidden camera. It's too much like a *Saturday Night Live* skit. I need someone to see this. This can't be for real.

My hot flashes begin to get flashier. "Can you ask someone else here if they know about the chicken?"

She does nothing. Blank face. Not a blink.

With sweat dripping down my back, I repeat the question.

She creeps over to the older, more veteran Carl's Jr lady in a hairnet and asks, I can only hope, my original question. Zombie Girl turns back to me and says, "It's a burger."

"So, like a patty?"

"Uh huh."

"Okay, I'd like to get a chicken burger with bacon and guacamole, wrapped in lettuce. No bun. That's it; NOTHING else on it. Nothing."

"So, tomato and mayo on that?"

I invoke my most hard-core stare. "NO. Okay, I NEED this to be right. It's important. Chicken patty burger with bacon, guacamole, wrapped in lettuce, no bun. Here are my notes. See them?"

I show her the notes and continue: "I was told that many fast-food restaurants do these and they are called 'protein style.' Can you do that for me?"

"Oh. Kay."

The exchange of money was more of the same slow-motion, blunted ridiculousness.

I was fully convinced this was not an intellectually challenged person; she just didn't give a crap.

"Here's your number," she said as she handed me a glossy flashcard that read 91. I looked around again. There was no one else in the joint.

I took a couple steps back. I wait. Maybe ten minutes. This is fast food.

"Number 91?"

"Yep, that'd be me."

Normally, not to offend, I would be more discrete when making sure an order is correct, but this time, not so much. I flagrantly open the bag right in front of Zombie Girl and unwrap the burger to confirm all has been done correctly. Praise the Lord, it has. It appears so anyway, but it is hard to tell without using my fingers to lift the "burger" and getting my germies on it.

I bring the burger to Stacie and inquire as to its quality. I specifically ask if it's a chicken burger patty and not a breast.

She says it's a breast. What she wanted all along.

Cart Before the Lord

There are two kinds of people: those who return their shopping carts and those who do not.

At the Irvine Spectrum shopping center, I had a couple of errands to do. First, to the Apple Store to exchange my iPhone for one that actually works, and after that, Target, to get a baby-shower gift.

Not completely thinking through the logic, I chose to park nearest the Apple Store to complete task number one, and then walked to the other end of the center to my second target, Target. After my successful iPhone exchange, it crossed my mind that perhaps I ought to drive my car down to Target to park again, but it seemed like so much work, so much redundancy, and it was such a warm winter's evening, the fresh air felt nice. Plus, how heavy can baby items be? Have you seen a newborn? Pulleese. They're tiny; what are they, like eight pounds?

Now in Target, I considered the items on the baby registry and decided to buy a car seat. That would be a nice gift for a nice friend.

After I nearly took out an elderly woman navigating the gigantic load in the snazzy Target cart (those puppies glide), I considered not only the wingspan but the weight. My car was so far away, this could present a problem: with the heft and girth of the box, surely this could not be carried. Yet I also really didn't want them to hold the box at the counter while I walked all the way to the parking structure to get my car, drove it back to Target, parked the car yet again, walked back into Target, retrieved the huge box, and schlepped it out to my car. So, in a momentary lack of virtue that I am not proud of, I figured—just this once—I could push the cart down to the parking structure and leave it, out of Target range.

This particular Target has an entrance/exit at one end that faces the parking lot, and another that faces the inside of Spectrum. Since the checkout was nearest the parking lot exit, I would need to push the cart on the sidewalk that runs alongside the outside wall of Target, and head back toward and into the Spectrum to get to the other side of the shopping center to get to my car. You might be asking, *Why do I care, Pam?* Let me tell you why.

As I approached the end of the Target, my cart stopped. Dead. I looked to see if it had gotten stuck on a pebble or something, and I could find nothing. *Huh, that's weird*, I thought. But it wasn't the first time I had picked a catawampus, mind-of-its-own cart in my shopping life, so I figured it had some underlying hidden issues.

Noticing that I'd just bypassed an altogether different, stranded cart, I thought, *Okay; I'll just transfer my load from this rogue cart and trade it for a better cart.* But the new cart would not move either. They would both move toward the Target entrance, but not away. What did these devil carriages have, GPS? Were there hidden cameras watching my shameless, cowardly act?

It was becoming a little more crystal: I had been outsmarted by a cart. Or The Man. Or both. Probably both.

I had a choice to make. I could accept defeat, push the cart back into Target, have them hold my purchase while I walked down to get my car, etc., but that would mean the last few minutes would have been wasted—and I am of the forward-thinking/acting persuasion. Rather than cut my losses and admit defeat, I thought, *Yeah, I can carry this box.* And so I did.

There were stares. I imagined what I looked like: just legs, hands, and box. I averted all eyes as I sweat and spit and muttered things under my breath. I'll admit it. I took short breaks, off-loading the box momentarily on things like a bench, a trashcan, a sturdy hedge. Eventually I could see the light at the end of that parking structure tunnel as I approached my bright, Target-red car.

When I am midway through doing a really dumb thing, fully conscious of the absurdity, sometimes I just don't want to quit. I'm committed to the dumb thing even when I know it's absurd, which makes it doubly dumb. But yeah, I had the satisfaction of hefting that gargantuan box on my own, wasting no time, repeating no steps.

Did I accept defeat? Did I ask for help? I did not. Yay, me.

There's a lesson in this—I just know it. I'm waiting. It's coming.

Sometimes God taps the brakes for me and says: *Are you sure you want to go this way? Is this best? You sure? Okay, do what you think you need to do. Sweat and spit and whatever, but do it on your own. Carry that weight; you'll get that satisfaction. You go, girl. I'll just be here.*

Chapstick

The midwives who surrounded the wailing, Viking-era Nordic woman, Aslaug, did all they could to help bring forth the baby, but of course they could only do so much. Off in the corner stood the power-hungry and bloodthirsty husband, Ragnar. Ragnar was a ruthless man, always fearless and often sadistic in battle. Yet in this moment he watched, wide-eyed, motionless, and silent—wildly out-of-character—with an utterly helpless, terrified face.

Breaking the tension from the History Channel television series, I offered my best Ragnar voice: "Chapstick? Chapstick? Honey, want some Chapstick?"

John smiled and instantly knew the reference.

It was 1986 and I was laboring over our firstborn, Joey. In preparation for this day, John and I had done Lamaze, learned about choosing a focal point, practiced the breathing techniques, made a checklist of all the helpful things to bring to the labor and delivery room, all the little tricks to help ease the pain.

As we left for the hospital, John excitedly grabbed the long-pre-packed bag with my clothing, toothbrush, and our tools from childbirth classes—things like a rolling pin for lower back pain, and Chapstick for my lips that would most assuredly be chapped. From all the screaming? I didn't know.

For some reason, in those weeks of Lamaze, the tool and tip that stuck out most in John's mind? *Bring the Chapstick.* Your wife *will* have parched, flaking, bleeding lips. And that's very bad. Offer the Chapstick. And offer the Chapstick often.

I loved that John was there for me, wanting to help—considering this was his fault. Even as I declined the Chapstick—when I was dilated at two centimeters, and then four, and then six, and fourteen, and so on—I thanked him each and every thoughtful time he offered the lip balm. I'm not quite sure though, at what point in my seventeen-hour labor (a seventeen-hour labor that included the baby Joey in a posterior position, which meant back labor, which meant the epidural WOULD NOT AND DID NOT TAKE) I'd had my fill of offers for the Chapstick. Finally, my one and only time of truly screaming during labor and delivery was at my Ragnar: "I DON'T WANT CHAPSTICK!!"

He didn't offer it again, and since then, Chapstick holds a tender memory for us.

The scene reminds me of times I felt helpless, frozen in my powerlessness to alleviate someone's agony. That's a hard place to be.

It reminds me of other times I was in emotional pain myself, and someone—trying to help—said a dumb thing and made my pain greater, making me feel even more isolated and misunderstood. Sometimes when we get uncomfortable with someone's pain, we get in the way of truly offering comfort by spouting pat answers. Churchy answers are the worst—demoralizing moralizing.

Job, a man from the Old Testament, had a Chapstick experience. Three of his friends, who probably had good intentions, kept shoving religious Chapstick in his face. Job faced mind-numbing, heartbreaking, unimaginable loss, and the way his pious friends attempted to help only hurt. His buddies thought they understood; they did not. Not having walked in Job's sandals, they handed out condescending explanations, questioned Job's faith, and reprimanded him, beating him down further. While some of their advice may have been technically true, they only worsened his suffering. They were not in it with him; they were on the sidelines.

I've done it too. I'm sure of it. Thinking I am wise, that maybe I do understand when I don't.

People like to hand out things. Like waxy wisdom sticks. Sometimes the only thing I can do—sometimes the very best thing I can do—is just show up. Show up and remember what we learned in class to help our beloved breathe.

The Intruder

Lazy Sunday afternoon. I was upstairs; John was downstairs.
"John! Hurry! Look outside by the pool! There's a wild animal!"

I watched the horrific creature saunter across the pool deck, headed for the heavy brush on the hillside. From my bedroom window perch, I watched John walk into the yard with his BB gun.

I jumped the gun and yelled, stupidly, "No, no, don't shoot it!"

"I'm just gonna warn it. So it doesn't come back," he yelled back to me.

Again, stupidly, I yelled, "NO! NO! NO!"

Doing an about-face and shaking his head, he walked back the way he came. "Alright." He holstered his firearm. The wild animal was now hidden somewhere in the lush brush of our back yard hill, nowhere in sight.

The next night, John was out of town on business. I was home alone and went to bed early. Ridiculously early, in fact. Before my elderly parents go to bed. And that's saying something about early.

10:30 pm Monday. Out of a dead sleep I sprung out of bed to the sound of a violent pounding. A scraping sort of pounding that seemed to be coming from the backside of the house, or maybe the back yard. I pulled the shade up a few inches. Before my now very wide eyes, I saw a dark figure and a flashlight peeking out.

My thoughts were rapid fire—*This is really happening right now. This is seriously happening to me right now. This is literally, right now, happening. To me. Someone is trying to break into my house.* I thought about the mini-ax I have in the bedroom drawer. Then I dialed 911.

"911, what is your emergency?"

I proceeded to calmly-ish tell the nice operator the nature of my emergency and I meekly asked if she would stay on the line with me until the police arrived. (I've seen in movies where they offer to do that, and since she didn't, I felt it was reasonable to ask. She agreed, which is really what matters in the end, although it would have been nice for her to offer. You see what I'm saying.)

With her still on the phone, I walked over to the bedroom door, opened it slowly (I know, bad idea. I should have locked it and barricaded myself), crept into the hallway, and from there I could see the same or maybe another flashlight through the downstairs windows on the front of the house.

I whisper-yelled into the phone, "I can see him in the front of the house!"

I could still hear pounding, and I worried that the intruder—I prefer "intruder" to "burglar," by the way, because burglar reminds me of the McDonald's Hamburglar, and this was no time for associating with a cartoon hamburger—might break in before the cops could get here.

That's when the doorbell rang. I thought, *What kind of intruder rings the doorbell?* It would just be my luck that I'd open it and there'd be a land shark behind the door.

"I'm not going to answer that," I told the operator.

"Yeah, I don't think you should answer that," the operator concurred. Clearly, she felt my instincts were solid.

I went across the hall to look out the front bedroom window and saw two cop cars in front of my house, which told me they sent backup, clearly indicating this was no joke. The two cops appeared to be talking to someone who sounded a lot like my neighbor Dave.

Feeling safer now, I said thank you and goodbye to the 911 operator. In my bare feet and wearing only my "More Cowbell" t-shirt and boxers, I went out front and greeted the police officers.

133

Although my view was partially obscured by the shrubbery and trees between our houses, I could see Dave a few feet away with his flashlight and baseball bat. I assumed it to be Dave, although for some reason I called him Mike. I was tired. And traumatized.

The cop seemed confused, "Is this your neighbor Dave?"

"Ah, yes, I meant Dave. Hey, Dave."

Apparently I had just saved Dave from being arrested.

Dave's version went like this: He heard a wild animal, which he said was a raccoon, thrashing about and sounding as if it was literally tearing apart and viciously devouring another animal. Dave was worried that the "raccoon" was killing our pet—our pet that we don't have. He came over to try and rescue our non-pet. Without calling first. While I was home alone.

Did I mention I was home alone?

I invited the nice, mustached, stiff-postured police officers to come take a look in my yard to see what we could see; perhaps we'd find the wild animal that Dave deemed a raccoon. Plus, they'd come all this way.

Walking through the house, one of the officers complimented the décor. "Why, thank you." I thought it was nice of him to notice.

In the yard there was no wild animal to be found, no carcass of a less fortunate animal, nothing. One cop even pulled up a chair to stand on and peek over the patio roof. "Looks all clear, ma'am," he said, just like in the movies. We called it a night, and the officers left.

Before going back to bed, I went into the kitchen to get a glass of water. My nerves slowly calming, I looked out the window, and right before my very wide eyes I saw the wild animal saunter-climb up the side of the house, back up to the roof/awning—and back to the scene of the crime.

His underbelly was inches from my face. To spite me.

I imagined that raccoon all self-satisfied, sitting up there on the roof gazing up at the moon, bloodied, dead prey at his side. Dressed in a Spiderman suit with a dark mask over his eyes, he'd have a flashlight on his lap and an ax at his feet. In one hand, a McDonald's hamburger, and in the other, John's BB gun.

Badpass

On hair-pinny, high-cliffy Highway 1, still south of our Big Sur destination, my husband Dario Franchitti—I mean, John Capone—attempted a pass maneuver. Just a moment before, gobbling my Trader Joe's Speculoos Cookie Butter with nothing but a butter knife, I had commented on the RV in front of us with its trailer full of colorful kayaks and other playful stuff: "Those are some fun-loving people, real Impracticals.[3] I might like to meet them.'"

Lord knows.

At that very moment, the light bulb over John's head, which makes the *vvaroooom, vvaroooom* sound, lit up as he decided this RV was going far too turtle-y for us to remain in tail. Seeing he was now fully committed to the pass, I remained dutifully silent as we launched into the oncoming lane. Without warning, the brake lights on the car *in front of* the RV lit up, as did their left turn signal. It became clear that this car was about to turn left into our lane, headed for a turn-out in front of us.

To recap: to our left, scary cliff; to our right, large RV. To add to this looming disaster, an entirely different car suddenly appeared in the oncoming lane, headed straight toward us. Four vehicles, not counting the funmobile's trailer with kayaks, all vying for the same stretch of road.

---

[3] I singlehandedly coined this term a few years ago, after a conversation that evolved into a debate with John about the merits of owning recreational vehicles like ATVs and boats. He said it was impractical to own these things considering cost, maintenance, storage, etc. Long story short, I won the debate. (Not that we own any of these things, but in theory, I won.) Simply, the term "Impracticals" is given to those who value fun.

John accelerated in an attempt to get in front of the RV, swerving out of the way of the oncoming car just as *that* rude car swerved away. Stunned, I looked in my rearview and saw the cars shimmying, still trying to regain control. I prayed that no one was about to join the choir invisible.

I may or may not have remained silent during that whole debacle.

Sometime later, after I regained calmishness, we pulled into a random vista point to our left—you know, to stop and smell the near-death. As we did, we saw the same RV with its colorful, fun stuff. Knowing I am never incognito in my little red car with the checkerboard roof, I heaved a deep groan of guilt-by-association and said something courageous like, "Oh my gosh, do not park near them. I feel awful that we almost caused that crash."

I stealthily ducked out the left side of the car and used its heavy metal as a shield against gunfire, just like in the movies. I looked over at John and saw his face aimed to the right, toward the funmobile. With a look of absolute, resolute conviction, almost illuminated by right action, he said, "I'm going to go apologize to them."

I said nothing. But as I watched him walk across the parking lot, all deliberate and poised, as if he were magnetized to the passengers in that RV, I remembered why I respect him so much. I could see him start to speak to the driver from a few feet away, identifying himself as the jerk who almost helped everyone die. I saw him shake hands with the man, his wife by his side. John, using humble body language, employed Italian hand/arm motions. I saw the woman put her hand on her heart as if to agree, *It was all very scary, but we're okay.*

I decided it was safe to walk over too.

As I joined the group, I got an instant vibe from the smiling woman that she'd be up for a huge hug. We embraced, and they both said kind, grace-giving words, adding that the guy who broke in front of them had made other dangerous and sudden moves, and that John had handled it all very well.

Basically, we were all victorious victims.

Turning back and waving as we walked away from our new, impractical friends, we were grateful it turned out this way versus us all becoming smashed-to-smithereens people butter.

Notes on lessons learned:
We might think we have skills, but we simply do not know what's around the corner.
Carpe diem. Have some impractical fun, but slow the heck down.
Life is short; eat the Cookie Butter.
Look to the right.
Own your stuff.
Step up.
Hug.

Brevity Levity

Rhetorically, the writer of the book of James in the Bible asks if we know what our lives will be like tomorrow. He compares our lifetime to a morning mist—here for a little while and then gone.

Thinking back to 2003, I kept a low profile when I accompanied my daughter to her registration for freshman classes at Mission High School. As much as I loved my mom, at that age it didn't take much to be embarrassed, and so it was that hindsight and wisdom that informed my own parenting style. My mom used to drop me off at school every day wearing pink rollers in her hair and her "housecoat."

Determined not to embarrass my own daughter, I dressed appropriately for Cassie's registration and inconspicuously accompanied her to the school. As we approached, a custodian was hard at work watering the flowers that outlined the concrete under the August sun. He pointed to the hose that was stretched across the quad and sweetly said, "Please be careful," to which I smiled and instantly caught my big toe underneath. This of course set things in motion for an Oscar-worthy stumble, complete with wild, flailing arms and an audible, "Oh, oh, no!"

I looked back at Cassie, poor thing. She shook her head.

I did feel bad about possibly giving the custodian a heart attack. I mean, he was up there in age, plus with that heat . . . But it's moments like these when you have to make a split-second judgment call. Sometimes a stranger has to take one for the team (the team being the collective "us"). The atmosphere in that quad was entirely too tense. And so I made the call and took the fall.

Joey reminded me recently that when I'd pull up in front of the school to drop him off, I'd roll down all the windows, open the sunroof on the Montero, and blast "The Macarena" while performing both the vocal styling and dance moves I'd seen in the Los del Rio music video on VH-1. As he reflected on those days gone by, he smiled. I can only interpret that warm smile as approval, as in, *Thanks for helping me adjust to high school. And life, Mother.* Hindsight again, rearing its thoughtful head.

It's not as though I enjoy embarrassing people or putting them in awkward positions—well, okay, I do enjoy that—but as I've told my husband, John, I'm an opportunity giver. I think it's valuable to see what would happen if I did this or that. It can be something simple and brief, a teeny moment. Like when a server lists Spaetzle as one of the specials of the day. Are you telling me you're not going to ask—with a straight face—about the "Spaetzle Special"? Please. I'll see it when I believe it.

On Saturday, John and I went kayaking with our friends Darren and Stacie. As we were just beginning our day, headed out from Dana Point Harbor, I had the idea to pull "The Great Wave Fake." (People in watercraft are just so friendly, always waving as if to say, *I see you there on your sailboat or your kayak or your paddleboard or your jet ski! This is so much fun that we're all here together on the water!* Why people driving in cars on roads don't have that same sense of community, frankly, makes me sad.) So I suggested, "Hey Stace, let's do this: Let's both raise our hands up over our heads as if we're going to initiate a friendly wave to someone, and then when they start to respond in kind, just scratch your head or point to a seagull or something." She, of course, was game. I think she'd played it before.

I didn't ask for these instincts. It might just be one of my spiritual gifts, like my spiritual gift of being able to determine whether a cake is moist from across the room, or the way I can tell if someone has chronic bad breath from up to twenty feet away based on if they're mouth breathers.

If part of my purpose on this earth is to be a facilitator—if I have to be the one to bring some levity to a tense situation, or bravely volunteer someone to be placed in an awkward situation to test their mettle, then all I can say is, I accept. Even if it's just for the "little while" that I've been given on this earth.

Hungry

Out of the three humungous fish tacos, I could only eat one.

As a reluctant member of the Clean Plate Club, I struggle with the whole wasting-food-guilt-thing. I have been known to bring home three gnocchi in a doggy bag. But this day, as we lunched on the shaded, wavy sand of Cabo San Lucas's The Office restaurant, taking my food back to the hotel was not an option. We were not going to be heading that way for hours, and it would surely spoil in the hot car. John and I briefly discussed what to do, wondering if we could give it to someone who might be hungry, maybe someone on the street.

When the server came, he asked if I wanted the leftovers to go. John chimed in, "Do you know if any of your friends might want it?"

Gulp.

I cringed at his wording, wishing he'd have said something more sensitive, something more along the lines of, "Do you know of any homeless or hungry nearby who might want it?" Anything but implying his friends—his peers—might need this food.

Without missing a beat, the server said, "I would like to take it home."

Bigger gulp.

After he walked away with my plate, my eyes welled up, deeply taken aback by his vulnerable answer. He could have responded by saying that he *knew* of homeless nearby; he could have saved his pride and still eaten it himself. He didn't even appear to consider that choice. He just humbly stated what was true: *He* was hungry.

A clean plate is overrated. Transparency is not.

Cup of Cold Water

I had just gotten home from Haiti the day before. As I brushed my teeth, I absentmindedly let the water run. Then I grabbed the faucet and switched it off, thinking about that water.

At the Redeemer's Child Orphanage in Port au Prince, we had just provided three days of vacation Bible school for more than 160 children—those who actually lived at the orphanage, as well as other street children who were invited to join in. Having split the children into three age groups, our team alternated these groups into three activities: games/sports, crafts, and a Bible lesson. I was the craft lady.

Most of the time it was semi-controlled chaos in a kind of stifling heat I had never before experienced. As the day wore on and the temperature climbed, I began to hear the same Creole word over and over: *dlo*. My translator explained this meant "water." More and more hands would tug on my arm and repeat "*Dlo*," and each time I pointed them to the well—a Sparkletts jug inside a nearby room.

Nearing the end of our craft session, a tiny boy, probably no more than four, pulled at my arm and pleaded, "*Dlo*." He looked as though he were ready to faint. I took his hand and walked him into the room, where we found pandemonium with children fighting over the spigot. His tired little body was no match for this mob, and he was getting trampled.

I picked him up and tried to muscle our way through, unsuccessfully, when I thought of another source and brought him to a room where our team had stashed our supplies and belongings. Offering him my personal water bottle, he grabbed it and chugged it all at once. As he handed it back to me he was instantly, magically, infused with new life, and a wide smile spread across his face. It was a radical shift. One minute he was completely parched and listless, and the next, hydrated and energized as though he'd just downed a twelve-pack of Red Bull.

Before my eyes, a basic need, an essential that I take for granted and waste while I brush my teeth, became a transforming illustration. Jesus tells me to give a cup of cold water to little ones, and because I did, I've seen what it can do.

The Bible lesson for me that day? We are all dying of thirst unless we drink the pure water, bottled at the Source.

Circles

"You're stupid," I heard the furrowed woman say to the child. I had just hopped onto an open-air city bus and was riding cable-car style, at the edge.

Interrupting her, I commanded, "Stop! How would you feel if you were a child, belittled by an adult?"

She sneered back at me, "Mind your own business! Who are you to tell me . . ." But then her raspy voice stopped short—and she seemed to have a change of heart. Smiling a reconciliatory smile, she reached out her hand as if to say, *Thank you; I understand now.*

She grasped my hand warmly, but as I looked down, I noticed she began to press a crooked, arthritic finger into my hand. Then, as she pulled it back up, I saw that the tip of her "finger" was the lit end of a cigarette, which she'd burned into my skin. I saw and felt the circular burn mark.

And then I woke up.

Yikes. Something's leaving a real mark.

Here's another scenario. Sometimes I imagine myself standing at the end of a dock over a still lake. I have a pebble in my hand. I look down; I drop the pebble into the calm water. The tiny rock hits the surface of the water, the water receives it, and there are concentric circles.

There is no alternative. What I touch, changes. For the good or the bad. My scuba-diving family tells me I cannot touch the ocean's coral because it is a living thing, and my touch will change it.

I love the character George Bailey in *It's a Wonderful Life*, probably my favorite movie. As a young man George is desperate to get out of Bedford Falls to make a name for himself and change the world. He wants not only a taste of the world; he wants a big bite, to devour it. Yet as George continually chooses to defer his own agenda to make way for others, he sees his dream dying and he is devastated.

Thankfully, in the end, it becomes clear that George did change the world standing on his dock. He thought he had to go out sailing the ocean. But he did it right from where he stood. George was satisfied.

In 2008, I watched my good friend Haydee pass from this earth. Haydee Del Cid Abel loved IMA with every fiber of her feisty Guatemalan being. She knew what kind of life Guatemala held for young girls, and she was compelled to make a difference. And she has; she does. Her touch continues there.

Haydee had asked me for years to visit her homeland with her, to become involved in her cause, but because I was distracted by my own life, it was not a priority to me. Finally, in 2008, when she was near death after battling cancer for five years, I went with Haydee to Guatemala. This would be her final trip home.

On that trip she mostly lay on the couch while her family and I took turns sitting with her, caring for her. She was in such pain. I remember how hard she wanted me to rub her head.

One afternoon she asked me to take her outside and give her a ride in her wheelchair. As I was pushing her tired, ravaged body, navigating the bumps in the pavement on the IMA campus, it was quiet. I parked her wheelchair in the sun, and from there Haydee pointed out the garden she'd planted and told me the names of the plants. She also talked about IMA and how the work needed to go on after she was gone. I told her that I would work for IMA.

She passed away a few days later.

Haydee's pebble made a wide, wide splash. Her circles continue. I pray mine will too.

Bijou under the Apple Tree

I stopped to get some flowers at Trader Joe's, because that seemed like the right thing to do.

When I pulled up to Stacie's house just before noon, I could hear voices in the side yard. So I peeked over and saw the gathering: Three men with shovels, dripping sweat, were digging a grave, and their counterparts—three ladies—were watching. I hadn't realized it at the time, but to my left, in the shade of the van tires, rested the well-made, homemade mini-casket that would be lowered into the earth.

The men kept digging until the depth and width felt right, and then they brought the box that said, "Here lies Bijou, 1-5-05—8-26-15." The lil' nine-pound Prague Ratter was only here a decade. Gone way too soon.

I had noticed on Facebook yesterday that people were posting pictures of their dogs because it was National Dog Day. Late last night, right before bed, I saw Stacie's post that her beloved Bijou had just died. *Oh no, not Bijou,* I thought. *Not now.* Stacie loves Bijou. Bijou loves Stacie. The whole family loves Bijou. I love Bijou. I've been spending a lot of time with Stacie and her dog the past couple of years, hanging out on the couch, Bijou jumping all over us like a puppy. Since Stacie's brain tumor diagnosis, we make time to be together.

It's my hunch that Bijou didn't want to be around for any goodbyes. Exit stage left.

Stacie's daughter, Maddie, said it was kind of good that the first time she had to experience someone close to her dying, it's Bijou.

With a clean white rope, the men lowered the casket into the ground, under an apple tree. Maddie took a single white rose from the Trader Joe's bouquet and placed it on Bijou's pristine pine box. The men picked up their shovels and began covering Bijou.

In other countries, I've noticed that the mourners remain at the graveside while the casket is lowered and dirt is placed on top. I'd never seen it in the States. So it sort of startled me at first—it felt too harsh to witness that part. But by the time the casket was covered, it seemed appropriate, like part of the acceptance process.

Some nice things were said about Bijou, and then we sang "Amazing Grace." Because it is. And because it felt like the right thing to do. For Bijou.

Budapest Ballast

When we moved back to California from our four-year stint in Utah, I asked John how long he thought it would be before we could buy another home. He estimated maybe six months. That felt doable.

Anyone leaving California and moving to one of the flyover states knows home-buying is much easier to do in their regions than easing back into the California market. We'd tried cutting corners by living in the tighter quarters of teeny condos but finally decided we needed more space.

I found an ad for a house for rent on Budapest Avenue. When we pulled up, we noticed the train tracks right behind the small back yard. The only thing separating the yard and the tracks was a few feet and a cinderblock wall. *That could be a problem,* we thought, *but we're here now, so let's give it a look.*

The homeowners, a lovely older couple, met us to show us their place. Let's call them Burt and Margie Cankle. Burt and Margie, who had to be in their mid-seventies, were just so warm and welcoming. John and I both thought so. With such an instant rapport, we felt they could be second grandparents to our kids. We even said it out loud. It just seemed serendipitous.

Walking through the 1,500-square foot house, we stopped in the master bedroom, which had a window to the yard. I leaned in and asked, with a just-between-you-and-me-tone, "Honestly, Burt, now how about that train track? How much of a factor will that be, you know, noise-wise?" He looked at me with wooly ears that were like Old Faithful geysers shooting out both sides of his head and, with sincere eyes, said, "Let me tell you, don't worry, Pam. It's nothing. Sure, you hear it once in a while, but you just get used to it. It blends in."

John and I looked at each other. It *was* a great price. I mean, we'd have more space; it was close to shopping, parks, and schools. There were just so many reasons to say yes. And so we did.

A few weeks later, we were exhausted but all moved in. I had fallen to sleep snuggled next to my husband that first night, grateful that the kids were all tucked into their own bedrooms for the first time in five years. It wasn't our own, but at least we had space. All was well. This was a good move.

And then, while we all slept like snug rug bugs, IT hit, with the same jarring quality as an earthquake in the black of night. But this was no earthquake. This felt otherworldly. My first thought was *Mother ship*.

A flashing, swirling, piercing light had invaded our bedroom while our ears rang with the most deafening, screeching din. We shot out of bed and looked at each other in terror, pacing around the room. We could barely hear each other scream. The clanking was horrific, like a tortured mechanical animal lamenting its death. Opening the blinds, I half expected to see little green men forcefully taking our new neighbors in their PJs into their spaceship. I hadn't even had a chance to say hello to them yet.

What we did see was a glowing monstrosity just over the top of the cinderblock wall, inching along on the train track, illuminating the midnight sky. John dashed out in his boxer briefs to get a closer look while I protected the children. Dragging a chair from the patio table, he peered over the side of the wall. He was now fearless, like Tom Cruise fighting the alien tripods in *War of the Worlds*. He came back in and yelled that he thought it was some sort of machine cleaning the tracks.

We wondered how often this would happen. Funny, Burt Cankle never mentioned anything about this.

After doing a little research, I learned that the ginormous train-track beast was called a ballast cleaner. *Ballast* in this context are basically crushed stones, and their purpose is to hold the wooden cross-ties in place, which in turn hold the rails in place, and the rails of course keep the train on track, which keeps us on track.

Thankfully, that was the first and last time we heard the hulking cleaner, but we never did get used to the freight trains all day and all night long the year-plus that we lived there. We tried to make the best of it, though. In the beginning, I had an idea: "Hey, whenever we hear a train, let's use that as a reminder to be thankful or say a prayer." There may or may not have been eyerolls. I was able to maintain that thoughtful, prayerful attitude the first couple of days myself, and then things deteriorated from there. Instead, I'd hear the train barrel by and say entirely different things.

Other issues arose, and Burt Cankle didn't turn out to be so much of a grandfatherly type. I don't want to say he was not a stand-up guy, or anything mean like that, but I will say I wonder if that shaggy black bristle spewing from his ears represented the blackness of his soul.

That's not nice; I take it back. Sometimes my heart needs a good scraping to keep me on track.

I've heard John refer to the ballast in sailing, and I'm no engineer, but ballast is anything that provides stability or weight. Ballast can take many forms. You're probably smelling the sweet aroma of a metaphor approaching, but it might be more than a metaphor.

There's emotional ballast, like my dream of owning a home again, as elusive it was. That six months turned into six years of wandering in the wilderness. I've treated my parents as my ballast, as well as my husband and my kids. I can't imagine anything more precious to me on earth than my family, but even they can't truly keep my equilibrium centered and okay.

We could all be snug rug bugs all tucked away, fast asleep, and a mechanical behemoth fireball can land in our yard. What we think might be our ballast might really be pseudo-ballast, and if that's the case, then we're never really stable. Maybe it's a job or a career or a relationship, a Facebook friends list, or that nut we just can't yet crack—that monkey on our back.

I think our ballast needs to be something pure and unchangeable. Something otherworldly.

Lab Work

The time is 7 am. The location is a muted lab waiting area in Southern California. Chairs are filled with groggy, hungry fasters with their heads bowed, reading their smartphones, waiting for their names to be called.

A diminutive Asian woman is first up. Shirley, the towering, husky-voiced African-American lab lady, begins to give her directions about the blood work, urine sample, stool—you know, the whole enchilada. Shirley narrows in on the stool instructions and refers to a stick: "Stick it in your stool in six different places."

I snicker; look up at the silent others. No one flinches. Sometimes you just want to tell someone where to stick it. Shirley gets paid to do it.

Shirley's so lucky. YOU KNOW when she goes home at night, she tells her husband funny lab stories. Far as I know, she's not held to any confidentiality agreement.

It feels good to tell someone where to stick it. For me, the good lasts about a minute. Then comes the stick-it remorse.

While I haven't technically used that phrasing, I have sent the message, good and strong. I can think of one fight over the elliptical at the gym. Okay, three.

Two out of those three times, I ran into those people again at the gym. That's a horrible moment. I got that gnawing feeling, my stomach starting to churn upward and bumping against my heart. It's called a heartchurn. After avoiding my adversaries, circling them a few times, and arguing with myself for a while, I finally walked over and apologized. Both times they accepted my apology, even though they were completely out of line to begin with, really. They both looked stunned when I said, "I acted badly. Will you forgive me?" Wide-eyed, they just both sort of nodded and said nothing.

Then there was this one time when I pulled a U-turn in a crosswalk and the lady in it completely overacted by reaching over with her closed umbrella and deliberately hitting the roof of my car. I have a *cute* car. And she wasn't in the slightest bit of danger. My car wasn't even that close to her—well, it technically was in the crosswalk, but her umbrella was ridiculously long. Dangerously long.

I hate to say sorry. I'd much rather eat a nice plate of Duck a l'Orange than a cold plate of crow.

But when push comes to love, I have a pretty strong righter-of-wrongs compulsion.

Barely teenagers, my friend Cheryl and I had been waiting patiently in line on the hot pavement for the sombrero ride (an alternative to the classic spinning teacups) at Knott's Berry Farm. Having gotten dropped off for the day by Cheryl's mom, we were feeling pretty grown-up, when a pack of girls—much larger in stature and probably older in age—indicated that they were about to cut in line. Cheryl wasn't having it. She immediately responded by blocking their moves, not allowing passage, and saying so in calm but steady assertions. I repeatedly gave her the what-are-you-doing-it's-not-worth-it stare. She wasn't having any of that either.

Cheryl continued to verbally engage with the pack while I stood silently by, thinking Cheryl a fool. But when one of them called my BFF an awful name, I got in her face without warning and belted out, "SHUT UP!"

Cheryl had that "Oh, no you didn't!" look in her eyes. They all looked at me like, *Where did you come from?* At that point Cheryl slunk back and I was the one in the verbal ring, blocking blows, throwing punches.

It was so long ago that the rest of it is a little fuzzy, but I remember the fracas lasting long past the sombrero ride, with those girls shadowing us for a few hours and taunting us in at least one other line by literally stepping on the backs of our heels. Thank God, that was the extent it got physical. By the end of the day, we had made friends. I won't say who saved the day.

Where a wise man once said turn the other cheek, my version occasionally goes, "Tell 'em to stick it where the sun doesn't shine." The good news is that the elliptical, the umbrella, and the Knott's Berry Farm dust-ups were many years ago, and I've grown up some.

Life is a laboratory. And we have our work to do.

Little Flower

I stood waiting at her door, listening to the sound of the unlocking of locks, and noticed the profusion of magenta and lavender in her walkway behind me.

When she finally got the door open, I bent down and embraced my precious four-foot-ten, eighty-six pound, ninety-two-year-old friend and said: "Inez, how lucky and blessed you are to be surrounded by these flowers. Do you just stand at your door and look out and think this is God saying 'I love you'?"

"Oh yes, yes I do," she smiled.

We hopped in my red Mini Cooper, which looks fabulous on her, and drove to Carrows for breakfast because they have that nice oatmeal Inez likes. Nursing a decaf, I had long finished my scrambled egg and wheat toast while Inez wielded a spoon close to the size of her head. Her silver hair and wide eyes barely peeking over her gigantic bowl of hot oats, we talked about things teeny and huge, deep and shallow. Now we were onto diet and fitness.

Inez was telling me about her routine, that she'll often eat oatmeal for breakfast but sometimes will alternate that as a dinner selection. I asked her what she likes to eat for lunch. Without missing a beat, Inez said, "I generally eat a yogurt, an Ensure, and a bunch of cookies."

I shot decaf through my nose. For three reasons: 1) She said this with a poker face; 2) I can identify with her quirky palate; and 3) this made me fall in love with her even more, and I didn't think that was possible.

My petite filet, Inez, is a meat-and-potatoes gal. On special occasions we'll go to a fancy steakhouse. After spending twenty minutes trying to convince her to go big since it's her birthday, she'll order the good steak and will then commence wolfing down the slab of beef and a plate of smooth, whipped-just-the-way-she-likes-'em, mashed potatoes. I once bought her a high-end whisk from Sur La Table because of how much she enjoys a smooth potato.

After our breakfast that day, I thought of something I wished I'd said at her door—something more accurate than what I'd said earlier. What I wished I had said is that those flowers are blessed and lucky to have her walk among them, and that maybe they hear God saying to them, "I love you, and Inez is a way I've shown you."

I'll have to say so next time I see her.

Capri Diem

John and I met Nancy, a nice older lady from Minneapolis. We had been sitting on a bench next to her on the island of Capri, astounded by the floral beauty and gazing at the turquoise Mediterranean surrounding us.

She had commented on something nice John had said to me, so we started chatting. Apparently Nancy struggles with eavesdropping, which is fine. I too am a "professional people watcher and listener." It's a calling. Not everyone's cut out for it.

Outside of being part of a tour group, Nancy was on her own, having left her husband behind at home. She'd always dreamed of traveling to Italy; he didn't want to. He thought he probably wouldn't like the food (hello, Ridiculous), but she came anyway. She said that both of her children recently fought cancer, and she now saw the value in seizing the day. She chose not to let someone else's limits or fear or discomfort stand in the way of living out her dream. In Positano we met Charlotte from Australia who did the same thing, and was traveling alone for a month. You go, girls.

One day on our vacation we didn't get around to doing something we'd planned on, and John said, "Well, there's always tomorrow." With my characteristic timing and *carpe diem* flair, I said, "Not always. Not on your last day."

I've learned this lesson in little moments not taken, so I'm a believer. I was doing a cardio workout on the beautiful, gazillion-step, rubble staircase from our hotel room in Positano down to the beach. I had been going up and down four times early each morning, and on my third trip down this day, I saw a couple of places I wanted to photograph. I thought, *I'll go back and get those shots on the next trip down. No sense going up to the room now.* But by the time I made the fourth trip, the lighting and sea currents had changed, the clouds had shifted, and what I had seen was gone. This moment had passed.

As they all do.

When Nancy returned to Minneapolis, and Charlotte to Australia, I hoped their husbands snuck a peek into their wives' photo albums, which captured the exquisite lighting of the clouds and the sea. And that soon after, the couples found themselves on a bench overlooking the Mediterranean, surrounded by flowers, with the breeze blowing through their loose, silver hair.

Little Miss Understood

It's 1992. From behind the lens of an 8mm Sony Handycam, John steps into the threshold of the master bathroom where he finds our three-year-old daughter Cassie, with what appears to be, a guilt-smile and definite makeup all over her face. Most notable is a vertical, deep red line down her left cheek and a daring lips application. An interesting choice. I'm not sure what she was going for with that line, and she clearly overshot things with the lips.

John/Daddy asks Cassie what she's up to.

Pointing to her lips, she says, "I was putting makeup on my wips." There is an effective dramatic pause between "my" and "wips."

"How come?" he inquires.

"Because I wanted some." *Hellllo, why do most women wear makeup?* To punctuate, she smiles and jumps up, clapping her hands.

"You supposed to be in Mommy's makeup drawer?" John probes.

"I din-din't." she says.

"You didn't what?"

"I din-din't go in Momma's makeup drawer; I just get makeup." She swings her hands, possibly as a distraction technique.

"But where'd you get the makeup?"

She points to the makeup drawer. Simple. "In here."

We hear the voice of her six-year-old brother, Joey. He piles on: "That's Mommy's makeup drawer . . ."

The camera pans and searches for Joey, finding him sitting on the floor a few inches away from Cassie. He's almost behind the door, tucked in. Joey's got a baseball glove in one hand and a ball in the other. He sees the camera on him and he chuckles, as if to say, *These kids nowadays! What are you gonna do?*

John asks Joey, "What do *you* think?"

With a contemplative face and a tone of *I don't want to be the one to say it, but . . .* He points to the drawer with his eyes, concurring with his dad, and says, "I think she went in there." *Et tu, Brute?*

"You do?"

"Uh huh," he says as he tosses the ball into the glove. He looks a little conflicted about his shifting loyalty and follows up a moment later with "Cas, you look pretty," and then a plea for "a game a catch" with Dad.

Ignoring his son, John says, "Cassie, I don't think you're supposed to get in Mommy's makeup."

She shakes her head, and with seemingly wild, lying eyes, says, "I din-din't."

He probes, "You didn't?"

"Huh uh. I get the makeup and then close it." She takes the time to demonstrate.

She seems to have legitimately confused her dad and he asks, "But isn't that the same thing as . . ."

"That's Mommy's makeup," Joey interjects.

Unmoved, she's like, *Let me clarify.* "I just get some makeup in that thing, in that big thing. Like that. Like this?" She scrunches her nose, moves close in to the camera

The dog and pony show continues ad nauseam with the threesome's respective agendas. John asks for a final time about the makeup.

"In that big thing, like that. In the drawer." Cassie again points to the drawer. She bats her eyelashes. She is the rock of Gibraltar.

"I was putting makeup on my wips," and looks at her dad with an *Okay, can we be done with this now?* face.

Eventually, they *are* done. Albeit a little Miss Understood, she is victorious.

I'd seen this video countless times over the years and conclud-

161

ed that it was primarily a nearly four-minute documentary of a child being caught red-faced and lying, never 'fessing up. It took me until just recently to see that Cassie was not the three-year-old with the wild, lying eyes. Pretty much from the get-go, she joyfully admitted she was putting makeup on her lips. But she seemed to contradict herself. In one breath she said she accessed the makeup, sure, but then when John asked, "Are you supposed to be in Mommy's makeup drawer?" she unequivocally states that she "din-din't." Something doesn't seem to be adding up.

One day not long ago, I came across the video, and the light bulb over my head flickered. I realized something we'd missed all this time: Cassie took John at his word—or question. She was not lying; she was simply saying, *No, I did not get into Momma's makeup drawer. I did not physically get* inside *her drawer. My body was not inside that little drawer. What are you, nuts?*

Having three years on his sister, Joey had "matured" out of hearing everything in a literal way. He was old enough now to miss the nuance.

The only real embellishment our daughter was guilty of was the smudged, scarlet makeup on her precious face. Joey was right: *Cas, you're pretty.* She was a literal little beauty, teaching us a twenty-three-year-old lesson we finally got: Dropping our agendas and assumptions, listening better, playing a game of catch, taking people at their word, is literally loving and loving literally.

Gold Dust

Driving down the freeway on an unseasonably scorching spring day, I kept time with a huffing and puffing, well-worn, dusty pickup truck filled with three men. Shoulder to shoulder, their tanned, veiny arms spilled out the sides of the opened windows. Hanging around the perimeter of the truck bed was a rack that held all the accoutrements—rakes, hoes, shovels, weed-whackers, etc., and in the bed itself, lawn mowers and blowers and bags of mulch and such. On the passenger side door was a magnetic sign that read in simple block letters: "Jesus Gardening Service."

On my car stereo at the very same moment, early Elton John sang, "He calls his child Jesus, 'cause he likes the name." Some might consider that a coincidence; I call these moments "Highlighters." You know, like Someone Up There is taking a big yellow highlighter to something to get my attention.

Jesus Gardening Service. I like the name. In this context, I imagine the pronunciation is "Hay-SOOS," but wouldn't it be just like Jesus to ride in a humble, donkey-like pickup truck? Right?

He'd never be in a self-indulgent, pimped-out stretch limo SUV—unless there was someone in there He wanted to talk to—but generally to get from point A to point B? He'd roll in a rusty, dusty pick-up . . . if I know Jesus.

Jesus as a gardener. It's not such a farfetched idea. After all, in the scene at the empty tomb, Mary mistook Jesus for the gardener. He had just asked her why she was crying and what she was looking for. Jesus tended to ask questions for which He already knew the answer. It was His thing. He's like, *I already know; I just want you to figure out what you know, and then we'll go from there.* For good growth, it's got to be organic and interactive.

There's rich, earthy soil, which is a living environment, and then there's just plain old dirt, which is basically dead soil. Dirty dirt.

Now, I don't know much about mulch, but apparently it's a key ingredient for effective gardening. Bare soil without mulch is the perfect place for weeds to grow. By covering soil with a layer of mulch, weed seeds have a harder time sprouting. And it's the organic mulch that interactively breaks down over time, adding nutrients, nourishing the soil while suppressing weeds. I have no green thumbs; I got the dirt on all of this thanks to Google. In fact, I struggle to keep silk plants from dying. That's why I need my gardener Hay-Soos.

Headed down Laguna Canyon, there is another well-worn pickup truck—this one always strategically parked for visibility and free advertisement, not far from where the day laborers hang out waiting for work. On the back of the tailgate is a humble sign. Above the name and phone number are block letters that read: "Dirt and debris call me." I see this truck regularly on the way to church, which is a dirt-and-debris removal place in itself, which is pretty perfect.

If I know Jesus, He takes my dirty dirt and turns it into gold dust.

Emptying Nest

Fall 2006:

"Do you want me to take the nest down?" John stood at the kitchen window looking out at the vacated bird's nest still perched in a nook of our back yard patio roof.

I shot back, "Are you serious? What if the birds come back and their home is gone?"

"I think once they leave, they leave. I don't think they return."

Absurd. I shook my head and walked away, sure that he didn't know what he was talking about.

I remembered the year before. Standing at our kitchen sink, I had a bird's-eye view of the nest building—how the expectant bird couple carried twigs to their spot and wove them into a home, one thin stick at a time. When it was finished the mother nestled in, and soon there were tiny white eggs under her wing. We photographed the bitty birds peaking through widening cracks in their shells, teeny wings gathering strength. We watched them take their first miraculous breaths. It reminded me of the nest John and I had built together, how hard we worked to make our house a home. As time passed, the chirping family outside the window mesmerized me—I could see clear parallels with our own. The timing was uncanny. The tender innocence was changing into something quite different: something loud and wild, crowded and messy.

I believe God took my face in His hands and pointed me to nature itself—another family in transition—as a way to say that the current turmoil in my home was not because of something I had done wrong, or because the kids were abandoning me. They were just growing up and out.

Early Summer 2007:

"There's someone here to see you, Pammy." John walked away from the front door suppressing a mischievous smile. I was too tired to be intrigued.

The visitors to our door often give away their identity—if it's Riley or Bradley, my three-foot-something neighbor boys who bring me untold joy with their hugs and ketchup breath, there's a minimum of a dozen rapid rings or door-knocker slams. But this time it was a non-distinct single chime. And I wasn't much in the mood for unexpected company.

I pulled my butt up off the melty couch, dragging myself up the steps from the den to the front door while I psyched myself up to be sufficiently polite—to whomever.

I looked through the doorway and saw a very large bird, nearly matching my height. This chicken standing before me was yellow and feathery and had a crimson beak. The left wing rose as if to say hello. I said, "This is a fine-looking chicken."

I didn't for a second have to guess the identity of this fowl friend. Intuitively, I knew this bird held the soul of my eighteen-year-old daughter, Cassie, who was heading to college soon.

Still standing in the doorway, I moved closer to look through the holes of the beak to see if I could make out blue eyes or blonde hair. I could not. A moment later Cassie decapitated herself, and my assumption was confirmed.

"I bought the suit to protest at KFC this weekend."

"Cool," I said to my little feathered friend who wears a chicken suit for my soul. And then she flew away.

Cassie left for the Pacific Northwest early on a warm August morning. Our son, Joey, had been gone for a while, making movies in Hollywood. John's car pulled out of the driveway too, headed for work.

Taking the stepladder out to the back patio, I reached above my head and reverently took down the dusty, cobwebbed nest. I carried it inside our home and placed it in a beautiful gold box and put it on my dresser, where it stays. Kept safe, treasured, loved.

Button a Button

It felt like we were going back in time as we passed through the dusty village of Cabaret. Getting more into the primitive country, we pulled off the main highway and turned onto a winding dirt road in the middle of a banana plantation. Port au Prince seemed a world away now. Riding on pack mules, natives carrying bushels of bananas watched as our SUV kicked up mud while we traveled down the winding path. Here, people bathed naked in a brown river, something I'd only seen in *National Geographic*. Now at our destination, we parked at the end of the road next to a small cluster of huts, tents, and makeshift shelters. All eyes were on us as we got out of our vehicle.

I was an orphan myself. While my personal story pales by comparison to the horrific reality of Haitian orphans, my experience that week visiting and working in the orphanages impacted me because of my own tender spot.

As we entered the dilapidated, sweltering building, we found maybe twenty unattended children in abject squalor. The older children stood catatonic, unresponsive to the younger children and babies who wailed. I've seen poverty in many parts of the world, but never have I seen the human condition in such a state, devoid of dignity. Our team of five women quickly scooped up the children.

Like most people, I've seen images on TV of developing-world children with the running eyes, bloated bellies, diseased skin, and bugs flying around and on them. It has always made me sad, but I was completely unprepared for how encountering it for myself would affect me when I touched their hopelessness. When I touched them, felt their skin, breathed the air they breathed.

As soon as I picked one child up, another one would plead to be held. The first one would then get jealous that I was holding another, and so the hitting began. There were always at least two more children standing on either side of me, pulling at my legs and arms to pick them up. All bawling. Some with clothes, many without. Toddlers lying lifeless on the ground, not a diaper in sight. Several children I'd picked up were wet. I'd try and shift them around, giving everyone a turn, but the crying never stopped.

Getting more and more overheated and overwhelmed, I looked around at my team members, and we all had the same desperate realization: we could not satiate them.

I had no idea how long we'd been there, but it felt like hours and I couldn't hold back my emotions. My crying turned to sobs, and I had to put the children down and exit the room to get some air. Once outside, I completely fell apart and to my knees. I started to cough and nearly threw up. I tried to buck up. I thought I was stronger than that. I just had no idea how unbearable it would feel to be in the presence of this kind of despair, unable to do anything to fix it. It shattered my heart.

I pulled myself together and was sitting on a ledge behind the building when a few children came near and climbed onto my lap. A little girl sat next to me, and it registered in her eyes that I'd been crying. She wiped the side of my face and tucked stray hair behind my ear. She patted my head. I looked at her and, without thinking, I began singing "Jesus loves me, this I know . . ." She watched my mouth and began singing it with me. More children came over and joined in, creating our own little choir. The melody felt like a balm on my heart.

I finally went back in to try and tend to the crying children and the team members I'd abandoned. One of the children I held was a toddler boy who had shorts on that were so big, they kept falling down and revealing his naked little bottom, so I just kept pulling them up. I needed to put the children down from time to time to rest my back, and when I did this time, the boy pointed to a buttonhole on his shirt that he wanted buttoned. I buttoned it for him and then took a look at his shorts to see if there was anything I could do to keep them up, when I realized a button was missing there as well. He wanted that shirt button buttoned even though his lower half was naked most of the time, shorts around his ankles as he walked around the room. It was as though he was saying, "Here, you can do this for me. My life is a complete mess but, here, you can button my button."

So that's what I did.

Seeing my need to comfort him, he comforted me.

The Dash

The dash is that line on your tombstone—the one between the year you got here and the year you left.

Meandering outside the city walls of San Gimignano, Italy, I spot a winding dirt path leading downward toward the lush, rolling hills of Tuscany. I am curious. Maybe a restaurant? I don't know. I could eat. It's been an hour.

Turns out it's a cemetery, a homeland of sorts. As I walk through the gate, an alarm sounds, so of course I go in. I look around. I think I might be in trouble. That's fine. Been there.

I see a tombstone with a name that thrills me to my core: "Craziella." Then I realize it says "Graziella." Even better. I may be crazy, but more than crazy, I'm grateful. Crazy grateful. Wish I would've known Graziella. I bet she was a juicy red tomato.

Walking through the cemetery, I am blindsided. My chest gets tight, eyes well up; I get a lump in my throat. I think of a friend who lost her mom this morning, and I pray for her.

My eyes are presented with names and actual photos on tombstones. Good lives, bad lives, I don't know. But no matter what, I bet someone loved them. No doubt these people resting with a view of Tuscany are remembered and missed.

I read the fabulous, excessive, extravagant Italian names out loud—names like Giovanna Capezzuoli Sardelli and Rocco Ricchetti—purposefully rolling my *R*'s, praying for the families left who are missing them, maybe still mourning.

I say names of people I have recently loved and lost:

"Elizabeth Simpson."

"Haydee Abel."

"Sue Wasko."

"Warren Johnson." It was coming up on a year without my brother-in-law, Warren.

I see spouses buried together, sometimes thirty years later. What were those years like without them? Thirty years later? That space, that hole. Did the one left alone let God fill that space? I hope so. I imagine my Italian parents, how they are together, so together. I imagine them without each other, even for five minutes. My chest gets tighter.

All of these people in this cemetery walked, spoke, loved, lived, died. All in that space of a dash.

I am stunned at how many fresh bouquets rest atop the graves.

John and I have plans to be cremated, with our ashes spread out over the ocean at San Onofre, near home. John, I may have a different idea now. I might want to be sprinkled over these rolling hills. Which means, if I go first, you'll get another trip to Italy out of that deal, so it's a win-win, right?

As I approach the gate to leave, a different alarm sounds, even more shrill. As I see the arms of the gate closing, I sprint, duck—dash.

I Love Lou

*S*itting on our couch with Lou, waiting for his *60 Minutes* show to debut, he was summarizing one of his stories with, "And the wind-up was . . ." This was Lou's way of saying, "When all is said and done . . ." or "At the end of the day . . ."

Lou has a way, period. He grabs hold of your heart. Even reporter Leslie Stahl knew it.

Last year we had Lou over to watch the show on our big screen. We rolled out a red carpet on our front walkway for his arrival, showered him with balloons and a plastic Oscar from Party City. Lou was one of a handful of seniors featured in the *60 Minutes* story about a groundbreaking study titled "90+." The researchers wanted to know what these ninety-plussers were doing right. Even among the handful featured, Lou was the phenom in the group. The guy could easily pass for twenty years younger.

Lou keeps your attention. Yesterday, John and I sat across from him with his barely gray, full head of hair and his "Freedom isn't Free" t-shirt at Mimi's Café. He has several versions of that shirt and baseball cap. He doesn't wear them to boast; he wears them to remind us that someone's paid for his freedom, yours, and mine.

We listened to his war stories over his celebratory ninety-fifth birthday mug of hot chocolate for breakfast—on a day that was 95 degrees outside. Lou served in WWII as a ball gunner in a B-17 bomber. Lou's not much more than five feet, but I suspect that his body is nearly all heart. It took a little big guy to get inside that dome and be the most vulnerable man on that plane.

Lou is well acquainted with vulnerability. Paraphrasing his favorite Book, I've heard him say, "There is no greater love than to lay down your life for a friend." After his plane was shot down over

Berlin, Lou spent eight months in a German POW camp. Last year we took him to the movie *Unbreakable,* the story of Louis Zamperini, the Olympic track star who had a brutal POW experience. Later in life, Lou had met Louis; they were peers with more than a first name in common.

After the credits rolled, we sat silent. I looked into Lou's face, and he seemed to be transported back to another time. I asked him what he thought, what he felt. As we sat there and listened to him talk in what I thought was an empty theater, I soon realized we weren't alone. There were a few stragglers leaning in. When they realized I was aware of their eavesdropping, I smiled at them like *I understand; he's pretty special.* I had a feeling they wanted to shake his hand but were reluctant to interrupt his story, so they just smiled a respectful "Thank you" as they quietly walked out.

A couple of weeks ago, we went to Lou's big ninety-fifth birthday party at the Laguna Woods clubhouse in the retirement community where he lives. It was packed. Rick Warren, author of the best-selling *The Purpose Driven Life* and Lou's pastor for thirty-five years, came to honor Lou. Pastor Rick meets with presidents, popes, dignitaries, and hangs out with people like Bono. And he hangs out with Lou. Lou's been an usher at Saddleback Church since its inception. I'm not sure there's a day that goes by that Lou isn't volunteering. Yesterday he said, "I volunteer because I don't want to waste my time."

I think you could say Lou's led a purpose-driven life.

Last year, John and I were Lou's special guests along with his daughter, Dolores, to the "Night of Heroes" at a local high school football game. Again, Lou was among a handful of special ones—WWII veterans—honored. Lou was a rock star that night, shaking hands, giving interviews, introducing John and me as his "family." I couldn't have been more proud. I heard the word over and over again: *hero.*

I've witnessed it countless times: If you call him a hero, he'll brush it off with a "Nahhh" and point to someone else. He'll say that the true heroes are the ones who gave their lives and those who came back from war severely wounded, losing limbs, their families, some losing their peace.

Freedom isn't free.

If you ask him the secret to his longevity, he'll give you that humble, sweet smile, probably shrug his shoulders, and say something like he did at breakfast at Mimi's: "God made me; he put me here . . . I don't know for how long . . ."

He's getting closer to the wind-up, when all is said and done. And the wind-up has been—for me—that I wound up being blessed in a big way by a little big guy who calls me family.

I love Lou.

Is This Thing On?

I killed it.
In the stand-up world, that's what you want to do, and I had. Coming off of a terrifying, but in the end, euphoric debut at the famed Comedy Store in Hollywood a couple weeks before, I figured a small venue in Huntington Beach would be like a sunset walk along the shore. It could only get easier, right?

My first mistake was thinking that this would be a small bar with a laid-back, half-lit surfer crowd. When I arrived, I found that Don the Beachcomber was roughly a frigillion times larger than the Belly Room at The Comedy Store. The place may not have been on Sunset Blvd, but it held three hundred and it was packed out, standing-room only.

Very quickly into my routine, I noticed people weren't laughing. They weren't even smiling. In fact, they looked confused. This was not optimal.

I continued, good little soldier I am. Then someone yelled, "We can't hear you!" and I realized my mic wasn't working. I continued to power through, sweat, tried to project my voice better, endured a series of brain fades, lost my place, was nauseated, and skipped around. Until finally I finished.

I had my "Is this thing on?" moment, and it really wasn't on. No joke. And no one came to my rescue. It was one of the loneliest and most humiliating experiences ever.

But the enormous room at Don the Beachcomber was not the toughest crowd. No, that would be the children in Haiti, months after the 2010 earthquake.

Something I noticed right away was that they didn't automatically reciprocate a smile. By contrast, when I go to the IMA School in

Guatemala, it's instant: I smile; they smile. Maybe not 100 percent of the time, but generally, easy smiles abound at the school. The IMA girls come from extreme poverty as well, but something was very different in Haiti.

I got the opportunity to work at a Haitian orphanage with a US-based group, One Love International (now known as HopeRoad Foundation). When I look at the snapshots of the kids there, I remember what it took to get those reluctant smiles. I put my back into it like never before—I crossed my eyes, contorted my face, did the monkey dance . . . You name it, I tried it. Sometimes none of it worked.

Haiti was already one of the most impoverished places in the world, and then when the catastrophic earthquake hit, it catapulted them even further in reverse. A child with a broken world probably doesn't feel a whole heck of a lot like smiling. Of those 160 children at our vacation Bible school, all were either residing there at the orphanage, or they were street children living in tents who came for the day. All had good reasons to hold onto their smiles. Not a lot seemed funny.

The evidence of the 7.7-magnitude earthquake was all around us—tent cities everywhere, roads that looked jackhammered, chunks of concrete, flattened buildings, crushed vehicles still in the road, twisted metal and building guts upended and strewn about like skeletons, a presidential palace in ruins. Nine months after the quake, it still looked like the island had imploded and no one knew where to begin to pick up the pieces. That's kind of how my heart felt while I was there.

I struggled with God in that place: *Do You see this? What are You doing about it?* What I saw kicked me in the stomach, and my questions to God stacked up pretty high as I wondered how something so broken could ever be fixed. It almost felt like the whole place had to be gutted somehow and begun again, from scratch.

At that time, Haiti had a 90 percent unemployment rate. Life expectancy was forty-eight. It was estimated that 350,000 people died in the quake, and that many bodies were still under the crumbled buildings. And living among the pieces of the broken city, surviving in tents and drinking contaminated water, were more than a million and a half people. Staggering.

I asked our guide for the week, Carl, what happens if there's a car accident and someone is injured, and whether there would be emergency services available. He said if there's an accident, you're on your own. You either get yourself to a hospital or hope someone takes you there. There's no one to call. Many people just die. The society's system, if ever there was a system, was completely broken by the quake. As for public restrooms, I saw men and women relieve themselves on the street. They had nowhere else to go. Literally.

I really wondered: Is this thing on? Does God hear? Is someone coming to the rescue when we're broken or alone?

I knew the glib answers we bounce back to someone who asks, "Where is God in all of this?" But none of those answers were working for me when I experienced Haiti. Then I began to think of Jesus' words where He says the brokenhearted are blessed with comfort. And isn't there this business all over the Bible about God turning our mourning into joy, our wailing into dancing, etc.?

That comfort, the joy, the dancing *must* be worth the pain. Right?

I brought Kahil Gilbran's *The Prophet* on that trip, and it was on the top bunk of that sweltering missionary house where I sweat and cried, reading it for the first time. The passage "Joy and Sorrow" is what confirmed my hunch about the Haitians' brokenness and their relief. Like in the words of Jesus, I heard a promise of comfort in Gibran's poetry, that the sorrow that was carved so deeply into these people—unfathomable gashes by a very real earthquake—could be matched and filled up, kind of like joy spackle.

But it can't just end there. There has to be more bang for that buck—because then it would be just a canceling-out kind of situation, like it all never happened; everything brought to zero. I think something happens above and beyond the spackle, like an outer coating, a glorious love sealer, and this is the Love Indescribable where we get to know our Healer. I think this is what Reinhold Niebuhr was talking about in the Serenity Prayer when he says, "Accepting hardship as the pathway to peace."

In my life I have cried as hard as I've laughed. But I first had to experience that excruciating, broken, vacant space to be filled with heaven-sent, inexplicable joy. For those stoic Haitian children, I don't know where or when, but I have to trust this is so for them as well. Otherwise, nothing makes sense. And nothing would ever be worth smiling over again.

Take the cannoli

My grandma had a reputation. Take her cannoli, for example. For years I've been on a search for a delicate cannoli shell like my grandma Annie Ciarolla used to make. There was only one other cook who came close, and that was Lena Bologna, a lady from my church. What a name: Lena Bologna. *Bellissima*.

I will say, Grandma may have had an edge just because, well, she's *famiglia*. But both Grandma and Lena made the best cannoli—not to mention gnocchi—I have ever tasted. They had the reputation, the one-two punch, of sweet and savory.

They've both long since passed, and I'm still trying to find the softer, gentler shell of my childhood—the one that melted in my mouth, lightly dusted with powdered sugar, with the chocolate chunks hidden in the white cream. The standard issue, even in Italy, is too thick and too hard. I've searched high and low, Como to Capri.

Hearing that Sicily is the birthplace of the tubular treat, I decided: if they can't do it, no one can. It's what they're known for. And so I went.

I'd seen *The Godfather* movies long before I had the privilege of traveling to Italy, and it was the funeral procession in *The Godfather II* that got my attention. The scene opens on a dry, rocky riverbed in the city of Corleone, which surprised me because I'd never imagined the landscape to be so arid, so bouldery and rough. It could put an eye out. Or a tire.

As we read the subtitles, we learn the backstory—that nine-year-old Vito's father had been killed for insulting the local mafia boss, and Vito's oldest brother, Paolo, had hidden in the hills in order to exact revenge. The band plays discomforting music while the members of the procession walk slowly, navigating the rough terrain.

Next, shots ring out and the cacophonous music stops while everyone scatters, and for a minute you think it's the wacky scene in *The In-Laws* when Peter Falk's character convinces Alan Arkin's to hit the deck, roll over, and then make a break for it by running back and forth to avoid getting gunned down. It also makes me think of Laurel and Hardy. Or the Three Stooges. It just seems out of place, Mr. Coppola.

Anyway, a woman in the distance starts screaming and the widow, Vito's mother, finds that her eldest son, Paolo, has been shot dead. Her son was killed at her husband's funeral. Now that's rough.

Long story short, young Vito eventually becomes Marlon Brando making all sorts of offers people can't refuse, and if they do, oh boy. Holy mostaccioli.

And yet, even the hardest bad guy can be soft inside.

There's a scene in the HBO series *Boardwalk Empire* featuring the character Al Capone and his sweet little boy, who's deaf and who can't be more than five. The delicate boy has been getting bullied at school and so Al is trying to toughen him up and teach him to defend himself.

Al, kneeling before him, says, "Hit me, tough guy. C'mon, hit me." He repeats it several times while his boy stares at him. The boy finally swings and misses, while Al continues to prod him.

He swings again and softly makes contact with his daddy's cheek. Al grabs his tiny hand and says, "What was that? C'mon, HARDER!"

Father shows son how to make a fist and tells him to protect his face as Al gets more physically and verbally aggressive: "C'mon, you gonna let people bully ya? C'mon, HIT ME!" he yells.

The boy's bottom lip pushes out, and he starts to whimper. You see it register on Al's face that he's unintentionally frightened his boy, and it's such a pure, private moment. He pulls his son to him as he says, "C'mere, c'mere." The child dissolves into his daddy, and his daddy into him. Al picks him up and starts to cry too. Rubbing the boy's back, he says, "Shhhh, it's okay, Sonny; it's okay." The boy burrows his head into his daddy's neck and Al kisses him and says, "Pappa's got ya."

Ah! That scene gets me every time! Even the nastiest, meanest, hardest guys!

John and I were in the city of Sircusa, Sicily, staying in a place that overlooked the Mediterranean with a view of the island of Ortigia—where, by the way, the apostle Paul of the New Testament preached. Sircusa is a brain-numbing, expansive window into ancient history. Along with the cannoli hunt, we had spent several days checking out the treasures of the early civilizations.

Wanting to see some of the best Greek ruins in the world (is that so much to ask?), we set out early in our Fiat 500[4] and headed to Agrigento's Valley of the Temples. These ruins are said to be some of the best-preserved ancient Greek temples in the world, even better than those in Greece. This massive archaeological site is what's left of the city of Akragas, a city founded by the Greeks in the sixth century BC.

Driving herky-jerky through a construction zone that looked an awful lot like that dry riverbed in *The Godfather II*, we were unable to avoid a jagged boulder in our lane and blew out our front tire. We were less than two miles from our destination.

---

[4] Fiat 500 tip: Get operating instructions before you operate this vehicle. It has an auto shut-off when you brake—even for a moment at a stop sign. At first we thought it was maybe a hybrid, and this was a gas-saving mechanism. We never quite figured that out. Just a lot of restarting in the least optimal places.

After the immediate *BOOM-flap-flap-flap*, John had no choice but to pull off on a no-shoulder, blindspot, hilly *S*-curve. On all fours, he struggled to put the spare tire on. After strategically placing reflective orange cones I'd borrowed from the nearby unmanned road construction, I authoritatively directed traffic from both directions. I just took to it. It was exhilarating and scary and fun all at the same time.

With cones back in place and the spare on, John contacted the rental place where we'd gotten the Fiat and, struggling through a hybrid language I call Spang-Eng-Ital, told them our situation.

The guy said we should take the car to the nearest Auto Europa to exchange it, but that was in Palermo, which was two hours across the island in the wrong direction, and John didn't think it was safe to drive that far on a spare. Our alterative was to replace the tire ourselves, but we were told we had to make sure we replaced it with the exact tire—a "Continental"—or we would have to pay a two hundred fifty Euro penalty, which was equivalent to three hundred fifty dollars.

Thus began the tire hunt. As nice as they were, no one at Tire Shop #1 spoke English. I whipped out my iPhone with its Italian-to-English and English-to-Italian translator app. Several Sicilians gathered around to help the stranded Americans and stare at my smartphone, but we couldn't explain to them how to speak into it so that we could hear the English translation. Kind of like that paradox when you've purchased a plastic-encased pair of scissors, but you need a pair of scissors to open the package. Finally, someone from across the street who knew a little English came over to translate, and we found out that, no, they did not have the Continental tire we needed, but they did give us vague directions to another tire shop in Agrigento that just might have the right tire.

Immediately after we finally found the second tire shop, *that* super-sweet mechanic told us they were about to take their lunch break, and you know what a "lunch break" in Italy is? Three hours. So we said we'd go to lunch too, maybe get a cannoli, and then head over to the ruins—our original destination—on the spare. It wasn't that far, so no problem. We said we'd be back in a few hours, after everyone was good and full.

With our stuffed bellies we walked the dusty, hilly paths of the Valley of the Temples in awe. So the day wasn't ruined.

Headed back to the second tire place, we found out that they also did not sell the Continental tire. This helpful guy had the idea of using Google Translate, so we communicated by typing our conversation into his computer. The mechanic typed, "You're on vacation. Just buy the tire and pay the charges," but Frugal John wasn't ready to give up quite yet.

Shaking his head, the guy told us the location of another shop that should have that brand, but there was no way to confirm since he didn't know the shop's name. Why no one knows the names of their competition in the same city, I found, well, interesting. After finding the third friendly tire shop, but no Continental, we cried *Zio* ("Uncle" in Italian) and bought a Pirelli from the man who was John's doppelgänger. John said he was tired of chasing a tire. At least this replacement tire would get us safely across the varied terrain of Sicily.

We finally hit the *autostrada* and headed to Corleone for dinner—the only reason being that it was Corleone and I wanted to say I ate dinner in Corleone. We bonded with the bosses, chatted with old men decked out in fedoras and ties who gathered on benches, ate dinner at a corner pizza place that boasted a neon sign with my mom's maiden name, and confirmed my building suspicion that Sicilians might just be the most go-out-of-your-way, kindest people I'd ever met. They have a soft shell and soft center.

The only rough thing in Sicily was the terrain that blew out our tire.

A few days later, having checked out of our hotel and returned our Fiat with our extra tire—and by that I mean, the one around my waist—we found out that we had gotten bad instructions and that our tire hunt was entirely unnecessary. Sure, we could have considered that wasted time, but we would have missed the opportunity to see Sicilians at their best, showing their soft inside. With that sweet satisfaction, we made our way to the Catania Airport to head back to Rome.

Across from our gate was, of course, a huge cannoli shop: I Dolci Di Nonna Vincenza. Just to be sure, John and I gave someone else's grandma a whirl. It wasn't a Lena Bologna or Grandma Ciarolla cannoli.

I didn't want to believe it, but it occurred to me that maybe the cannoli shell is supposed to be hard. Period. I'd tasted cannoli up and down the mainland of Italy, and now all over Sicily. We'd been chasing an idea of a Continental and a cannoli. Maybe neither existed.

Maybe it was Lena's and Grandma's special touch—their own spin on the original that got that soft shell.

Or maybe it's the Creator who helps get the holy in the cannoli.

Pure Honey

Without so much as a hello, and with a thick Russian accent, the spiky-haired Costco lady saw my two large bottles of honey, narrowed her eyes at me, and said: "You like honey? You use that much honey?"

"Yes."

"Vwhat you use it for?"

"Tea . . . smoothies . . . recipes . . ."

"Vwhat, you don't like agave?"

I wasn't even sure what agave was. I couldn't say that, what with her so serious about her agave.

I felt my eyes dart around. I shrugged and shook my head. She had rattled me.

I felt a little guilty knowing I was buying so much because I like the way the sun shines through it in the tall glass jar on my counter. I do use it for tea, though. It's not the healthiest kind on the market, so when I'm going for health, I dig a spoon in the "other" honey—the one that's in the cabinet, down below. Notice I said dig, not dip.

Honey's all the rage these days. It's made a comeback similar to turmeric, kale, and Brussels sprouts—some of our trendier, fashionable plants. Honey's supposed to have loads of uses and can cure what ails you, they say. Okay, so I buy in too; I've succumbed to the hype. Got a cough or high cholesterol? Have some honey. A spoonful of honey used to make the medicine go down. Now the spoonful of honey *is* the medicine. Some say it always has been. Even King Solomon told his son to "Eat thou honey." John the Baptist had a little locust with his honey. I prefer a little on a baguette with walnut and Gorgonzola.

The thing is, from what I understand, the raw, unfiltered, stiffer, cloudy stuff, like the Manuka I get from New Zealand, is the best for you; it's not the silky golden kind I buy at Costco. That stuff is heated and treated and has been around the block several times. The little Manuka jar, however, is so expensive you'd think it's real gold. In summary, the honey I don't love—taste-wise—is the one that's got all the primo health benefits. Figures.

As a kid, I'd heard the name *Pamela* meant "Sweet as honey." I didn't buy it. I'd wished it had a different meaning, something a little edgier like Sheena, Queen of the Amazon or Xena, The Warrior Princess. (For what it's worth, I also wished I had a one-to two-inch slightly diagonal/mostly horizontal scar just below my right eye so that I'd look rogue. I also put tin foil on my teeth to make pretend braces.)

I just looked my name up again to see if what I remembered is true, and it said in the original Greek it means, "Honey; all sweetness." Well, I can tell you right now, that's a load.

If we're going to talk about sweet names, the one that comes to mind is Jesus. I remember singing an old hymn in church that had the line, "Jesus, Jesus, Jesus, sweetest name I know." I loved it. I've got to tell you, I don't like when Jesus' name is used as a curse word. It's so common, and the worst possible way to use His name. There are just so many better ways to invoke His name, like asking for help, for example.

The prophet Isaiah in the Bible described Jesus as pretty ordinary looking, maybe more like the unfiltered, raw Manuka that's good for you. Isaiah said He had nothing about Him that would make us notice Him, no handsomeness or physical attractiveness that would draw us to Him. In other words, people weren't doing double takes at him because he looked like Angelina's Brad. He wouldn't have made *People* Magazine's Most Beautiful list AD 27.

He likely didn't resemble the paintings we've all seen, or the actors who've portrayed Him. Once, my son and I were in a doctor's office waiting area and saw a long-haired, bearded, extremely handsome young man sitting in a chair waiting for his name to be called. Joey and I spied him at the same time, looked at each other, and mouthed, "Jesus."

People would not have been attracted to the real Jesus by His dashing good looks. They were attracted to him for His healing properties.

There were also those who weren't attracted to Him at all—those who hated Him so much they killed Him. What they failed to see is that He's the best medicine of all.

The Mermaid Tale

Getting in my car in basically my jammies, I hit the 5 before five and beat the early-morning Los Angeles traffic. I'd packed my toiletries and clothes I'd need for my commercial audition in Hollywood and was getting myself ready at the Sunset Boulevard 24-Hour Fitness, above the Archlight movie theatre. Standing in front of the mirror applying mascara, I tried to tune out the annoying static from the television perched in the corner of the locker room ceiling. When the static suddenly faded, I heard the voices of LA newscasters report that this morning would be the first of a four-day free health care clinic at the Los Angeles Sports Arena, and that people who had gotten wristbands earlier in the week had camped out and were waiting their turn to see a doctor or a dentist. A sadness washed over me, thinking about the people on the street who had no other alternative.

I thought about how that could have been me. I thought about how, as complicated and different as we all are, we have so much in common, such similar needs. At the very least, we need our teeth cleaned, and it would be nice to have our cholesterol checked. We're the same. It's just us.

I thought about that summer night in 1988 when John and I, along with our two-year-old Joey, attended an event at that same sports arena. As we got to our car, a man approached us and humbly told us he was hungry and really needed something to eat, and asked if would we help him. This wasn't a first for us, but for some reason, the tender way he asked—the sound of his voice—touched John and I so much that neither of us could get him out of our heads that night as we tried to sleep. So much so that we ended up getting involved in ongoing work with the homeless after that.

After I finished getting ready for my audition, I still had some time to kill, so I headed to a McDonald's. Judgmental types might think I should have outgrown McDonald's by now. I haven't, okay?

After I ordered my OJ and sausage biscuit with cheese, no egg, I selected the only booth available. I was literally surrounded by people who were talking to themselves, and it wasn't that they had a Bluetooth in their ear. They all appeared to be street people with mental illness. And none of them had any food that I could see.

I felt so bad that I couldn't eat. I didn't know what to do. I felt guilty for throwing my food away, but I didn't want to compromise their dignity by offering them my food, and I wasn't sure if I should approach any of them and ask if they needed help, since they weren't asking.

The next night I had trouble sleeping, and so I got up and checked my email. I had gotten a note from a friend/cousin, Nancy, who told me about an experience she'd just had, unaware of the one I'd had the day before.

She'd taken her daughters, Gia, six years old, and Mila, three, to a favorite hamburger joint for dinner. After they'd finished eating, Nancy followed her girls outside to the huge sculpture they love to play in (it's actually probably supposed to be a whale, but they call it The Mermaid Tail.) This time though, there was a young woman inside. It was getting dark out, so it was a little hard to see, but Nancy said the girl was probably early twenties, had three backpacks, a few books, and an orange juice. And she was twitching, like maybe she had a speed problem.

Not expecting to see an adult inside the mermaid tail, the girls were naturally inquisitive. Mila asked what her name was (Tina), and this began a sweet conversation. Nancy said there was an "unspoken knowing" between the girl and her that she was homeless, but the girls hadn't a clue. They just thought she was a nice girl inside a mermaid.

Gia asked her why she had so many bags, when Nancy cut in and said, "Gia, we always have a ton of bags too. I'm always carrying your stuff everywhere . . ." and then wrapped things up by telling them that they needed to get home because their 8:30 bedtime was approaching.

They said goodbye and started to walk away when Mila looked back and asked Tina, "We are going home now. Are you going home too?"

"Pretty soon, I hope," Tina said.

When they got into the van, Nancy had an achy feeling in her heart. Tina was so young, and she could see that she was a sweet person.

Strapping the girls into their seatbelts, she said to her daughters, "I want you to know that the girl inside the mermaid tail is homeless. She doesn't have a home to go to, and that's why she has all those bags."

Gia kept asking questions about her and said that they should go back and get her and bring her home and feed her. And let her sleep in their guest room. She pleaded with her mom, "Let's go back and bring her food."

When they got home, Gia was taking off her shoes and asked, "Where is her mom? Where is her family?" In the email to me, Nancy wrote, "And then she started to cry. My little Gia."

Gia came up and hugged her and said, "Momma, I feel so bad for her. She is so young and she doesn't have anyone to help her . . ." Six-year-old Gia whispered into her mommy's ear, "She is just too young."

Nancy was flooded with regret, wishing she had said something to Tina like, "Looks like you are traveling. Can we go and grab you something tasty at The Habit?" She wished she had offered her *something*.

Tina was so sweet to the girls. Nancy didn't want to belittle her, though. She repeated my thoughts from the day before in McDonald's: Sometimes you just don't know if you should offer something. Especially when you're not asked. Nancy assumed Tina didn't ask because the girls were so awesome to her and they were "treating her like anyone else in the world."

Because she is. It's just us.

I'm guessing that was a milestone—a marker—for Gia. My hunch is that Gia became slightly less innocent having encountered Tina, who was "just too young." But in Gia's own words, there is a revelation for me that she innately knew that this was just too much, and Tina was far too young to be without her mommy, her family, her home.

As we all are.

Reading Nancy's email, a different sadness washed over me. It was kind of a beautiful sadness because it was mixed with the appreciation of how it impacted Gia—that she was so moved by the girl in the mermaid tail. And this, I believe, she will never outgrow.

REI

I got my REI dividend check in the mail. It was for $6.50. Somebody is definitely trying to tell me something. Clearly, I'm not spending enough at REI.

Some people believe the universe sends us messages. I would agree if, by *universe*, they mean God specifically.

When I am less distracted, I get more messages.

When I shut my mouth, I get more messages.

When I'm in nature, alone, I get more messages.

When I stop trying to figure things out, when I stop trying to conduct the orchestra, when I travel and see a new or a favorite place, when I'm on a road trip by myself and the radio is off, when I talk to teeny children, when I talk to precious long-timers, when my ears are not "clogged with gnocchi," when I pay attention and, sometimes, even when I don't pay attention and am caught off guard, when I'm humbler, when I am broken-openhearted, I get more messages.

From God.

I have never heard an audible voice. But I have heard His voice.

Spread out over my fifty-three years, I've had three dreams where I've experienced a force and a power and a spirit I cannot describe. There simply are no words available. What I know for sure is that they were heavenly, and I mean that in the most real sense of the word. I cannot describe the beauty of the experiences, but I can tell you what they were: a peek and a taste and a touch of heaven.

Each time one happened, I awoke with a mind-blowing, momentary clarity and understanding, but also a sadness that I could not stay there. My sadness dissipated as I relished the knowledge that these moments were promises of more to come. And one day, I won't have to leave them.

The most recent one was just a month ago.

After each of these experiences, I thought they were so magnificent, so life-changing, so unforgettable, that they would sustain me in living as a new woman. I've tried to write them down, just in case. But like I said, there are no words, so my writing stinks. Over time, they fade. They always have. They slip away a little more each day. But I still know that they happened.

From what I can tell, this is a common problem. If you go back to Bible times, people would literally see all sorts of supernatural events—what were called signs and wonders. The people knew these miracles were from the Creator, the Almighty, but over time they forgot. They went back to living pre-miracle, pre-sign, pre-wonder.

There is some evidence that these things spoil people, that they can become addictive, with their witnesses needing them to be able to believe. Doubting Thomas was one who said he must touch the holes in Jesus' hands and side in order to believe His Master had risen. Jesus Himself observed: Thomas, you believe because you've looked upon My wounds with your own eyes, but the greater blessing is for those who believe without having to see Me first.

When I was eighteen months old and given a home when I needed one, it became the most defining experience of my life. By that I mean, everything hinged on that event. I was a rescue. It was the first act of grace that I could always point to—the first one that I was aware of, at least. It poured the foundation for my life, a platform on which I could stand, as wobbly as I was.

When I was twenty-eight years old I had a series of fortunate events over the course of a few months that collectively relayed the same message—one that I was previously unable to hear. I had struggled with long-term wobbliness that affected my hearing, a kind of spiritual vertigo. I finally heard; I finally stood straight: I was created by a loving God, and because of that very fact, I was beloved by Him.

From that point on, I was good to go. I mean, for a while. I still tend to want more reminders that I'm okay. I'm spoiled too. Yet I've gleaned a few more things:

I'm not special.

I've earned none of the grace I've been given. Still, I'll take it.

God speaks anywhere He wants, and He can use anything He chooses. A gardener's humble truck, an overlapper on a plane, a subway musician, a little boy who needs his button buttoned, a self-inflicted black eye. The more you believe it's possible, the more it is.

Bookend

I love what St. Augustine said about the world being a book—and I'm really lucky I get to flip through a few of those chapters with John. We just got back from another "just for fun" adventure. With no real autumn to speak of in Southern California, we typically head east in search of fall, specifically to the Catskills in upstate New York.

In our red Kia Soul rental this year, we began our drive up Palisades Parkway and away from Manhattan. Sometimes a point of contention between us is how fast John drives, but this time, he *took his time.* I heard him whisper, as though it didn't matter if anyone was listening, "It's too nice of a road to speed through."

Not only did we find fall, we found more and more evidence of a loving, creative God who seems to give us those brilliant colors just for fun, for our pleasure, for proof—if we are willing to truly open our eyes and heart.

I, of course, documented these findings with my iPhone camera. As an exercise in déjà vu, I came within inches of losing it in the Mohonk Lake, this time snatching it in the knick of time, the way a wide receiver catches a pass on the football field. It was epic. All of it.

Oh, and we also go to New York for the food—for the closest thing to Italy itself.

John's a guy who will let me drag him all over the NYC subway system on a quest to find the most authentic homemade pasta in Brooklyn. So after several transfers, we left the subway station and walked down Withers Street, heading toward the little place Pasquale Bamonte opened in 1900. Taking in the local color, I looked up and saw an elderly woman leaning on her elbows on her windowsill, looking out into the street, eyeballing us. Just like in the old country.

Sometime later, with our bellies satisfied, we departed Bamonte's. Waddling back toward the subway station, I saw the same woman still in her window, looking out directly at us. John noticed I was staring back at her and asked, "Are you two people watching?"

"Yes," I replied, motioning toward the woman, "She's a colleague."

At JFK getting ready to board our flight to LAX, John noticed I was looking back, carefully watching a woman setting up her supplies, preparing to clean the restroom. Apparently, John's my people-watching protégé these days. Smiling, he asked, "Dot connecting?"

"No, I'm still gathering data. Dot connecting is my night shift."

Acknowledgments

Big love and thanks to all those grace-givers who have helped me get here. My biggest cheerleader is my husband, John, who has believed in me always—all ways—and who agreed to take on the coveted moniker, "Personal Literary and Publishing Assistant to Ms. Capone." I sometimes call him my backup brain, but in reality he's often my main brain. There are also the obvious, key people like Joey and Cassie and other close family and friends who have said, "Rah rah, you can do it!" who I could not possibly mention all by name, but there were those random, semi-unbiased cheerleaders—people like Sean Marshall, Tina Sechrist Randy, Lucy DeCaro, and Chuck Marlatte whose encouragement truly pushed me over the edge to begin this book. I can't explain it, but for some reason, it was those voices that had no skin in the game who made me get on the field after years on the sidelines.

Helping provide blurry details for some stories were John Capone, Mike Capone, Vanessa Capone Watson, my kids Joey and Cassie Capone, and my parents Joe and Jean Ciarolla.

A gigantic, couldn't-have-done-it-without-you thank you to my incredibly patient, meticulous, and talented team, who made me look good:

Kris Bearss, editor

Tony DeCaro, graphic design

Glenn Harmon, cover and interior art

Wayne Hastings, publishing consultant

Robert Kazanjian, author photo

Thank you to Radford Sechrist, who led to Glenn, and Nancy Jernigan, who led to Kris.

For miscellaneous, invaluable help—Jeni Olsen, Christopher

and Andrea DeCaro, Lucy Decaro, and all those early endorsers/blurb writers, voters, re-Tweeters and other social media promoters—Robyn Henk, Kirsten Mickelwait, Dee Eastman, Jim McNeff, Terri Green, Tina Sechrist Randy, Sean Marshall, Janice Mock, Cheryl Johnson, Beth Midgley, Amy Koenig, Nancy Revis, Jamie Grant, Dennis Carlson, and Patricia Johannsen. And anyone I somehow forgot due to my sleep deprivation, or anyone who helped after this went to print . . . forgive me, and I thank you from the tip of my bedhead to the tips of my toes.

PS: I know virtually nothing about football (apart from the fact I do have a decent arm), so if any of my football analogy is off in the first paragraph above, I will, as usual take the grace.